STUDY GUIDE

for

Nutrition & You

JOAN SALGE BLAKE

Created by
Charlene Harkins, EdD, RD, LD, FADA
University of Minnesota Duluth

PEARSON

Benjamin Cummings

San Francisco   Boston   New York
Cape Town   Hong Kong   London   Madrid   Mexico City
Montreal   Munich   Paris   Singapore   Sydney   Tokyo   Toronto

Publisher: Frank Ruggirello
Development Manager: Claire Alexander
Acquisitions Editor: Sandra Lindelof
Assistant Editor: Emily Portwood
Managing Editor: Deborah Cogan
Production Supervisor: Mary O'Connell
Manufacturing Buyer: Dorothy Cox
Marketing Manager: Neena Bali
Cover Photograph: StockFood Creative/Getty Images Inc.
Supplement Cover Designer: 17th Street Studios
Main Text Cover Designer: Jeanne Calabrese
Design and Composition: The Left Coast Group

ISBN-10: 0-321-49803-8
ISBN-13: 978-0-321-49803-8

Contents

Chapter 7
Vitamins   124

Chapter 8
Minerals and Water   159

Chapter 11
Nutrition and Fitness   250

Chapter 12
Lifecycle Nutrition: Pregnancy through Infancy   266

Chapter 13
Lifecycle Nutrition: Toddlers through the Later Years   295

Chapter 14
Food Safety and Technology   310

Chapter 15
Hunger at Home and Abroad   331

Answer Key   342

Preface

This Study Guide is a companion to *Nutrition and You* by Joan Salge Blake. Completing the activities presented here will help you to better understand how to apply the material presented in the textbook to your daily life, and will help you highlight areas where you may need to improve your eating or shopping habits to live more healthfully.

The Study Guide includes five activities per chapter section:

The **Know It** and **Find It** activities will help you understand and use important terminology. Activities include matching exercises, word games, crossword puzzles, and choosing the right answer.

Think About It presents a brief scenario that a college student is likely to experience. Most of these questions or activities have specifically desired answers.

Apply It activities are personal self-evaluation and assessment tools. Activities in this section will ask you to evaluate your diet, your shopping choices, and your eating out behaviors. You will also be evaluating menus, meal plans, and nutrient needs.

Test It has multiple choice questions that would be suitable for use in an exam. These are mostly recall-based questions to check if you're remembering important terms or concepts from the chapter section.

Additionally, the Study Guide asks you to interpret the **Two Points of View** opinions featured at the end of each chapter in your textbook. You will need to read critically to determine if you agree with the experts—and more importantly, why or why not.

Read each textbook chapter, then complete the activities in this Study Guide. You can check your answers with the Answer Key located at the end of the book.

Read It. Study It. Do It. Enjoy It!!

1 What Is Nutrition?

What Drives Our Food Choices?

✓ Know It

Match each term to the appropriate description.

_____ 1. the measurement of energy

_____ 2. conversion of food to energy

_____ 3. chemical compounds in food

_____ 4. nonnutritive compounds in food

_____ 5. the science of how chemical compounds affect health

a. phytochemicals

b. kilocalories

c. nutrients

d. metabolism

e. nutrition

✔ Find It

Listed below are reasons why we choose foods. Put the following factors or foods under the reason that best describes why you would choose to eat a food item.

| salty pretzels | instant mashed potatoes | Got Milk | chocolate |

| environment | prewashed vegetables | bagel for breakfast | rice as a staple |

| holiday dinner | bond with others | rotisserie chicken | breakfast cereals |

celebratory meal

Taste and Culture	Social Reasons and Trends	Time and Convenience	Advertising	Habits and Emotions

✔ Think About It

1. It is Friday afternoon. You have just finished a midterm exam and feel like celebrating the end of the week. If you invite a few friends to your apartment, this would be an example of

   _____.

2. You stop by the grocery store on your way home to purchase pizzas that are advertised at four for $10. This would be an example of choosing foods for _____.

3. One of your friends doesn't eat meat, so you make sure that one of the pizzas is topped only with cheese. This is an example of accommodating your friend's _____.

✓ Apply It

1. What was the last food advertisement that you came in contact with?

   _____

2. Where did you hear or see this ad?

   _____

   _____

3. Was this advertisement for a food item that could be considered healthful? Why or why not?

   _____

   _____

   _____

4. Would you purchase this product? Why or why not?

   _____

   _____

   _____

✓ Test It

1. An example of a food trend is
   a. eating cereal for breakfast.
   b. heat-and-serve frozen entrées.
   c. commercials for fast-food salads.
   d. eating with family members.

2. It is impossible to successfully market fresh fruits and vegetables.
   a. true
   b. false

What Is Nutrition and Why Is Good Nutrition so Important?

✔ Know It

Match the term with the appropriate description.

_____ 1. the science of nutrients and their effect on health

_____ 2. the relationship between nutrition and gene expression

_____ 3. sequencing of DNA in all human genes

_____ 4. contains the genetic material

_____ 5. processing of genetic information to create a protein

a. gene expression

b. Human Genome Project

c. nutrition

d. nutritional genomics

e. DNA

✔ Find It

Put a check mark next to all diseases that have a nutrition-related component.

_____ kidney disease

_____ cancer

_____ stroke

_____ accidents

_____ influenza

_____ heart disease

_____ diabetes

✔ Think About It

1. The cafeteria lunch choices are chili con carne, chicken fingers and french fries, or a bacon, lettuce, and tomato wrap. Which lunch would you choose if you were trying to select heart-healthy foods? Why?

   _____

   _____

   _____

2. The beverage choices are diet soda, lemonade, or iced tea. Which beverage would you choose? Why?

   _____

   _____

   _____

✔ Apply It

1. If it were possible for you to have your genetic material analyzed to find out whether or not you would develop some form of cancer, would you want to know this? Why or why not?

   _____

   _____

   _____

2. If the results were positive (you would be likely to develop cancer in your lifetime), what would you do differently right now?

   _____

   _____

   _____

3. If the results were inconclusive (unknown), what would you do now to avoid a chronic disease later in life?

_____

_____

_____

✔ Test It

1. Good nutrition plays a role in reducing the risk of

    a. diabetes and influenza.

    b. accidents and Alzheimer's disease.

    c. respiratory disease and blood poisoning.

    d. heart disease and stroke.

2. Deoxyribonucleic acid

    a. is an essential nutrient.

    b. contains energy.

    c. contains genetic instructions.

    d. creates specific proteins.

What Are the Essential Nutrients and Why Do You Need Them?

✔ Know It

Fill in the blanks below using these terms.

organic   inorganic   calories   micronutrient   macronutrient

1. Carbohydrates, lipids, and proteins are called _____ because they are needed in high amounts in the diet.

2. Vitamins and minerals are considered _____ because they are needed in lesser amounts.

3. Food energy is measured in _____.

4. Because they contain the element carbon, carbohydrates, lipids, and protein are all

   _____.

5. Minerals are _____ substances.

✓ Find It

Complete the chart below.

Use X to mark each nutrient that provides energy; provides for growth, maintenance, or structure; helps regulate body processes; or contains carbon. One box has already been checked for you.

	Energy	Growth, Maintenance, or Structure	Regulate Body Processes	Carbon Containing
Carbohydrate	X			
Protein				
Fats				
Vitamins				
Minerals				
Water				

✓ Think About It

1. Using your age, gender, and activity level, it is possible to estimate _____.

2. The energy nutrient with the most calories per gram is _____.

3. If you wanted to increase the number of calories your body needs, you could _____.

✓ Apply It

A food label provides the following information per serving: 14 g carbohydrate, 2 g protein, 4 g fat, 200 mg calcium.

1. How many calories are there in a serving? _____

2. Which nutrient provides the most calories? _____

3. What percent of the calories are contributed by the carbohydrate? _____

✔ Test It

1. Nutrients that yield food energy include
   a. carbohydrates, vitamins, and lipids.
   b. carbohydrates, protein, and minerals.
   c. lipids, protein, and minerals.
   d. carbohydrates, protein, and lipids.

2. The most calories would be yielded by
   a. 10 grams of carbohydrate.
   b. 12 grams of protein.
   c. 8 grams of fat.
   d. 1,400 milligrams of sodium.

How Should You Get These Important Nutrients?

✔ Know It

Match the term with the appropriate description.

_____ 1. carbon containing	a. fiber
_____ 2. minerals, water, salts	b. inorganic
_____ 3. indigestible parts of plants	c. organic
_____ 4. speeds up body reactions	d. phytochemical
_____ 5. nonnutrient healthful substance in food	e. enzyme

✔ Find It

Use this figure to answer each of the following:

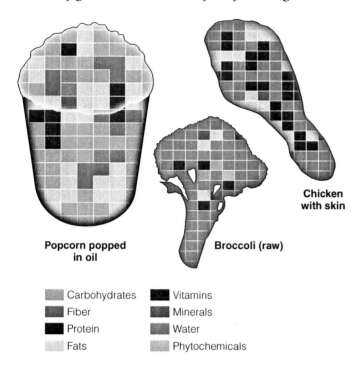

Popcorn popped in oil

Broccoli (raw)

Chicken with skin

▨ Carbohydrates		▨ Vitamins	
▨ Fiber		▨ Minerals	
▨ Protein		▨ Water	
▨ Fats		▨ Phytochemicals	

(Refer to page 12 in your textbook for a full-color version of this image.)

1. The most prevalent macronutrient in the popcorn is _____.

2. The most prevalent macronutrient in the raw broccoli is _____.

3. The most prevalent macronutrient in the chicken leg is _____.

4. The food item with the most vitamins and minerals is _____.

5. The food item with the most fiber is _____.

6. The most phytochemicals can be found in _____.

✔ Think About It

1. If you wanted to increase the fiber in your diet, you could _____.

2. If you wanted to decrease the fat in your diet, you could _____.

3. If you were concerned about taking in too many calories, you could _____.

✔ Apply It

Consider what you had for breakfast today. What was the major source of calories in this meal?

_____ Which macronutrient provided most of this energy? _____

If you wanted to increase the amount of phytochemicals that you have at breakfast tomorrow, what food

items would you add? _____

Why? _____

✔ Test It

1. Fiber can be found in all of the following except

    a. meat products.

    b. fresh fruits.

    c. vegetables.

    d. whole-grain bread.

2. The six classes of nutrients include carbohydrates, protein, _____, vitamins, minerals, and _____.

    a. fat, fiber

    b. lipids, water

    c. phytochemicals, enzymes

    d. fiber, water

How Does the Average American Diet Stack Up?

✔ Know It

Check each of the following that is part of the goals or objectives of Healthy People 2010.

_____   increase life expectancy

_____   improve quality of life

_____ increase health disparities among segments of the population

_____ promote good health

_____ increase body weight

✔ Find It

The average American takes in a high amount of some nutrients and a low amount of others. Put each of the following nutrients under the category that would be characteristic of the typical American diet.

sodium   vitamin E   fiber   calories   calcium   saturated fat

Low	High

✔ Think About It

1. What is an epidemic? _____

2. Why is obesity being termed an epidemic? _____

✔ Apply It

1. What food items do you regularly consume that you think are too high in sodium, saturated fat, and

   calories? _____

2. What foods could you choose in place of these items? _____

3. What factors would make you choose one food over another? _____

✔ Test It

1. *Healthy People 2010*

    a. is a set of health objectives for the United States.

    b. is a set of health objectives written by the World Health Organization.

    c. specifically targets minority health care initiatives.

    d. is specific to obese adults.

2. Most Americans need to focus on

    a. eating fewer carbohydrates.

    b. avoiding dairy products.

    c. eating more protein.

    d. eating more fruits and vegetables.

What's the Real Deal When It Comes to Nutrition Research and Advice?

✔ Know It

Match each term to the appropriate description.

_____	1.	method used to generate research findings	a.	laboratory
_____	2.	an idea based on observations	b.	experimental
_____	3.	opinion of a group of experts	c.	placebo
_____	4.	experiment involving animals	d.	scientific
_____	5.	looking at factors to see relationships	e.	epidemiological
_____	6.	population research	f.	control
_____	7.	group receiving treatment	g.	observational
_____	8.	group given placebo	h.	consensus
_____	9.	sugar pill	i.	hypothesis

✓ Find It

1. Where would each statement on the right fit into the scientific method diagrammed on the left?

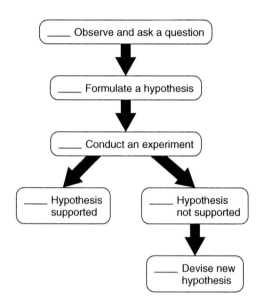

a. Eliminate vending machines from campus housing
b. Eating snacks from vending machines causes weight gain
c. Students gained weight
d. Why do college freshmen gain weight?
e. Watching TV causes weight gain
f. Students stopped gaining weight

✓ Think About It

Researchers were interested in knowing if the flavor of a beverage had an effect on the amount of fluid consumed by active people. The researchers observed a large group of active people during exercise sessions in a laboratory setting. The subjects did not know the intent of the research. They were under the assumption that the researchers were interested in how well they could run on a treadmill.

The subjects were randomly divided into two groups. One group received water during exercise. The other group received a flavored beverage to consume during exercise. Because both beverages were clear, the researchers did not know which beverage each subject was given.

1. This type of research is an example of _____.

2. The placebo group received _____.

3. The experimental group received _____.

4. What would you hypothesize as the outcome of this research?

_____

_____

✓ Apply It

Find a newspaper article that describes a nutrition-related finding.

1. List the source, title, and date of this article.

    _____

    _____

2. Is the article headline descriptive of the research presented?

    _____

    _____

3. Can you tell if this article is reporting the results of a peer-reviewed journal article? How?

    _____

    _____

    _____

4. Where could you go to find out more information about the reported finding?

    _____

    _____

    _____

✓ Another Apply It

Do an Internet search using the key words "Nutrition Research." Select one website to examine. Answer the following questions.

1. Who runs the site?

    _____

    _____

2. Who pays for the site?

_____

_____

3. What is the purpose of the site?

_____

_____

4. Where does the information come from?

_____

_____

5. What is the basis of the information?

_____

_____

6. How current is the information?

_____

_____

7. What is your overall impression of this website? Why?

_____

_____

✔ Test It

1. The first step in the scientific method is to
   a. conduct an experiment.
   b. formulate a hypothesis.
   c. ask a question.
   d. come to a consensus.

2. Gathering health statistics of 10,000 people living in New York City is an example of _____ research.
   a. laboratory
   b. case study
   c. observational
   d. epidemiological

Two Points of View

Food Advertisements: Help or Hindrance

Read two professionals' opinions on this topic at the end of the chapter in your textbook, then consider the following questions:

1. "What we put into our own mouths ought to be our own business." Do you agree with this statement? Why or why not?

   _____

   _____

   _____

2. Do you think advertising increases brand loyalty? If so, give an example. If not, why?

   _____

   _____

   _____

3. Do you think advertising affects food preferences or choices? If so, give an example. If not, why?

_____

_____

_____

4. Which expert, Radley Balko or Margo Wootan, do you most side with in this debate? Why?

_____

_____

_____

5. Suggest advertising techniques that could be used to increase consumer purchases of fruits and vegetables.

_____

_____

_____

6. How would you know if your advertising was effective?

_____

_____

_____

2 Tools for Healthy Eating

What Is Healthy Eating and What Tools Can Help?

✓ Know It

Match each term with the appropriate definition.

_____ 1.	inadequate nutrition	a. overnutrition
_____ 2.	long-term consequence of poor nutrition	b. undernutrition
_____ 3.	excess nutrients or calories	c. Dietary Reference Intakes
_____ 4.	recommendations for nutrient needs	
_____ 5.	a food guidance system	d. *Dietary Guidelines for Americans*
_____ 6.	broad dietary and lifestyle advice	e. malnutrition
		f. MyPyramid

✔ Find It

Check all of the following that are examples of overnutrition.

_____ excessive intake of iron

_____ too many calories

_____ avoiding dairy products

_____ consuming animal products

_____ drinking sugar-sweetened beverages

✔ Think About It

In reviewing your food choices for the past few days, you realize that your staple foods have been bagels, ramen noodles, frozen pizza, and an orange-flavored drink. This menu could be an example of

_____.

✔ Apply It

1. Write down what you have eaten so far today.

   _____

   _____

2. What particular nutrition concerns do you have?

   _____

   _____

3. What can you choose to eat for the rest of the day that will help to balance out your earlier food choices?

   _____

   _____

✓ Test It

1. An obese person could be malnourished.

    a. true

    b. false

2. Of the following, the most helpful tool for menu planning is

    a. the Dietary Reference Intakes.

    b. the *Dietary Guidelines for Americans.*

    c. MyPyramid.

    d. the National Academy of Sciences.

What Are the Dietary Reference Intakes?

✓ Know It

Match each term with the appropriate definition.

_____ 1. reference values for the essential nutrients	a. EAR	
_____ 2. approximate amount of a nutrient that groups of similar individuals consume to maintain health	b. RDA	
	c. DRI	
_____ 3. average amount of a nutrient; meets the needs of 50 percent of the individuals in that group	d. AI	
_____ 4. meets the needs of most people in a similar group	e. AMDR	
_____ 5. highest amount of nutrient consumed without harm	f. toxic	
_____ 6. harmful level	g. UL	
_____ 7. healthy range of intakes for energy-containing nutrients		

✓ Find It

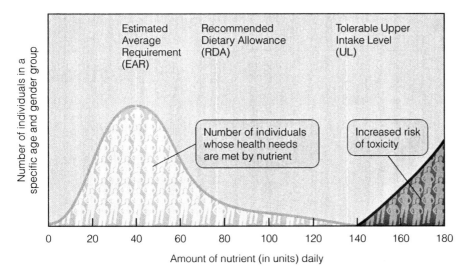

(Refer to page 30 in your textbook for a full-color version of this image.)

Looking at the figure here, determine the numerical value of each of the following:

Recommended Dietary Allowance (RDA) _____

Tolerable Upper Intake Level (UL) _____

Estimated Average Requirement (EAR) _____

Toxic level _____

✓ Think About It

You analyze your diet using a computerized program and discover that 40 percent of your calories come

from fat. This means _____.

If you want to decrease the percent of calories from fat, you could _____

_____.

✓ Apply It

1. Look at your last grocery store receipt. How much money did you spend on food items? _____

2. How much of this was healthful spending? _____

3. How much of this was spent on junk food? _____

4. What specific changes will you make when purchasing food next week?

_____

_____

✔ Test It

1. The EAR is generally higher than the RDA.

    a. true

    b. false

2. The _____ is the starting point to determine the amount of a nutrient that individuals should consume for good health.

    a. EAR

    b. RDA

    c. AI

    d. AMDR

What Are the *Dietary Guidelines for Americans?*

✔ Know It

Match each statement to one of the Dietary Guidelines *listed below.*

_____	1. Consume less than 10 percent of calories from saturated fat.	a. Adequate Nutrients within Calorie Needs
_____	2. Properly clean, prepare, and store food.	b. Weight Management
_____	3. Maintain balance between calories consumed and the amount needed for a healthy body.	c. Physical Activity
_____	4. Give three two me, please.	d. Food Groups to Encourage
_____	5. Consume a variety of nutrient-dense foods.	e. Fats

_____ 6. Choose lean dairy products, whole grains, fruits, and vegetables.

_____ 7. Avoid processed foods.

_____ 8. Try to be physically active every day.

_____ 9. Consume alcohol in moderation.

f. Carbohydrates

g. Sodium and Potassium

h. Alcoholic Beverages

i. Food Safety

✔ Find It

Many of the Dietary Guidelines _have overlapping recommendations. Note all of the guidelines that address each of the following concerns._

a. Adequate Nutrients
   within Calorie Needs
b. Weight Management
c. Physical Activity

d. Food Groups
   to Encourage
e. Fats
f. Carbohydrates

g. Sodium and Potassium
h. Alcoholic Beverages
i. Food Safety

_____ 1. Maintain a healthy body weight

_____ 2. Eat more fruits and vegetables

_____ 3. Increase physical activity

_____ 4. Include low-fat dairy products

✔ Think About It

Breakfast
Oatmeal
   with brown sugar and cream
White bread toasted
   with butter
Tea with lemon

Lunch
Cream of chicken
   wild rice soup
Soda crackers
Diet soda

Dinner
Bean burrito
Refried rice
Beer

1. Look at the menu listed above. Does this menu meet all of the _Dietary Guidelines for Americans?_ If not, what is missing?

_____

_____

2. What suggestions do you have for this menu? What menu items would you take out or substitute? Why?

_____

_____

3. What food items would you add? Why?

_____

_____

✓ Apply It

Fill in this Food Frequency Questionnaire for yourself.

Food Item	At Least Once a Week	At Least Daily	2–4 Servings Daily
citrus fruit			
green leafy vegetables			
dark orange fruit or vegetable			
whole-grain product			
low-fat dairy product			
legumes, beans, or nuts			
whole-milk dairy product			
high-fat meat products			
fried food			

Compare your chart to the *Dietary Guidelines for Americans.* Do you need to make any changes? If so, what would they be? If not, why not?

_____

_____

_____

✔ Test It

1. The *Dietary Guidelines for Americans* have specific recommendations for

    a. folate and iron.

    b. junk food items.

    c. sodium.

    d. weight-reduction plans.

2. Carbohydrate-rich foods include

    a. chocolate, nuts, and ice cream.

    b. tortillas, hummus, and milk.

    c. chicken, peas, and mashed potatoes.

    d. bacon, lettuce, and tomato.

What Is a Food Guidance System?

✔ Know It

Match the appropriate phrase with the concept.

_____	1. relationship of one food group to another	a. moderation
_____	2. amount of nutrients per calorie	b. discretionary
_____	3. reasonable, but not excessive	c. proportionality
_____	4. different foods, different food groups	d. variety
_____	5. making small changes over time	e. food guidance system
_____	6. visual diagrams to help with menu planning	f. nutrient density
_____	7. calories left over once nutrient needs are met	g. gradual improvement

✔ Find It

Complete this chart.

Food Group	Calorie Dense	Nutrient Dense
Grains	cookies, pastries	
Vegetables		fresh and frozen
	canned in syrup, drinks	whole, 100% real juice
Milk	ice cream, cheese	
Meat and Beans		eggs, lean meat, dried beans and peas

✔ Think About It

You are in the habit of eating a snack in the morning between classes. Most of these snacks come from a

vending machine that is stocked with chips, candy, and gum. Generally, these foods lack _____.

Food groups likely to be missing include _____.

✔ Think About It More

Table 2.2

What Is Moderate and Vigorous Activity?

Do you know what exercise is moderate and what is vigorous? Check your assumptions below.

Moderate Activities Expend 3½ to 7 Calories a Minute	Vigorous Activities Expend More Than 7 Calories a Minute
Brisk walking	Jogging or running
Bicycling 5 to 9 mph	Bicycling more than 10 mph
Shooting hoops	Playing competitive sports like basketball, soccer, or lacrosse
Using free weights	Rowing on a machine vigorously
Yoga	Karate, judo, or tae kwon do
Walking a dog	Jumping rope

Adapted from Centers for Disease Control and Prevention, *General Physical Activities Defined by Level of Intensity*. Available at www.cdc.gov.

Using Table 2.2, answer the following questions.

1. Which of the following would burn the most calories?

    _____ lifting free weights for 20 minutes

    _____ jogging for 15 minutes

    _____ jumping rope for 10 minutes

    _____ walking a dog for 45 minutes

2. Label each of the following activities with **M** for moderate and **V** for vigorous.

    _____ swimming more than 30 yards per minute

    _____ downhill skiing

    _____ hip hop dancing

    _____ a game of rugby

    _____ canoeing at less than 2.5 mph

    _____ playing baseball

    _____ recreational volleyball

✔ Apply It

Complete the Self-Assessment below.

Does Your Diet Have Proportionality?

Answer yes or no to the following questions.

	Yes	No
1. Are grains the main food choice at all your meals?	☐	☐
2. Do you often forget to eat vegetables?	☐	☐
3. Do you typically eat fewer than three pieces of fruit daily?	☐	☐
4. Do you often have fewer than three cups of milk daily?	☐	☐
5. Is the portion of meat, chicken, or fish the largest item on your dinner plate?	☐	☐

Answer

If you answered yes to three or more of these questions, it is very likely that your diet lacks proportionality.

1. What have you learned about your diet?

   _____

2. What diet changes do you plan to make?

   _____

Table 2.3
How Many Calories Do You Need Daily?

The amount of calories that you need daily is based upon your age, gender, and activity level.*

	Males				Females		
Age	Sedentary*	Moderately Active	Active	Age	Sedentary	Moderately Active	Active
16–18	2,400	2,800	3,200	18	1,800	2,000	2,400
19–20	2,600	2,800	3,000	19–20	2,000	2,200	2,400
21–25	2,400	2,800	3,000	21–25	2,000	2,200	2,400
26–30	2,400	2,600	3,000	26–30	1,800	2,000	2,400
31–35	2,400	2,600	3,000	31–35	1,800	2,000	2,200
36–40	2,400	2,600	2,800	36–40	1,800	2,000	2,200
41–45	2,200	2,600	2,800	41–45	1,800	2,000	2,200
46–50	2,200	2,400	2,800	46–50	1,800	2,000	2,200

*These calorie levels are based on the Institute of Medicine's Estimated Energy Requirements from the *Dietary Reference Intakes: Macronutrients Report,* 2002.
Sedentary: Partaking in less than 30 minutes a day of moderate physical activity in addition to daily activities.
Moderately Active: Partaking in at least 30 minutes and up to 60 minutes a day of moderate physical activity in addition to daily activities.
Active: Partaking in 60 or more minutes a day of moderate physical activity in addition to daily activities.

Source: U.S. Department of Agriculture, MyPyramid. Available at www.mypyramid.gov.

3. In Table 2.3 above, circle the amount of daily calories recommended for you based on your age, gender, and activity level. Does this seem like a realistic recommendation? Why or why not?

   _____

   _____

✔ Test It

1. Controllable factor(s) that affect your calorie needs include

    a. age.

    b. gender.

    c. activity.

    d. race.

2. The best way to make use of the MyPyramid food guidance system is by

    a. using an interactive CD.

    b. accessing the website on the Internet.

    c. using the textbook.

    d. using handouts produced by the Dairy Council.

3. The most nutrient-dense food in the following list is

    a. a baked potato.

    b. french fries.

    c. potato chips.

    d. sour cream mashed potatoes.

What Is a Food Label and Why Is It Important?

✓ Know It

Identify information that can be found on a food label. Find and circle the words listed below.

CALCIUM
CALORIES
CLAIMS
FAT
FIBER

INGREDIENTS
IRON
MANUFACTURER
NAME
PROTEIN

SERVING
SUGAR
WEIGHT

```
Y  C  K  Q  A  O  G  Q  N  R  I  M  A  Y  C
S  E  I  R  O  L  A  C  Y  N  T  A  O  W  F
G  G  Z  P  V  Z  I  J  G  D  A  N  S  X  B
N  C  N  O  I  B  T  R  K  S  F  U  O  I  M
O  K  L  I  D  W  E  I  G  H  T  F  N  U  D
N  O  C  A  V  D  E  M  A  N  V  A  I  F  J
H  A  A  J  I  R  M  Z  L  C  F  C  E  I  M
G  N  I  E  N  M  E  R  D  I  L  T  M  V  G
S  G  N  D  I  Q  S  S  B  A  S  U  S  K  B
N  T  B  I  E  C  R  E  C  S  I  R  F  S  O
S  O  X  J  T  W  R  I  L  U  O  E  S  S  L
P  S  R  N  O  U  M  M  G  G  T  R  I  D  U
V  F  D  I  R  E  X  Q  N  A  L  Y  F  W  K
P  X  Y  U  P  R  C  F  S  R  A  E  C  E  M
G  S  E  K  G  V  O  Z  D  D  T  K  M  Q  Z
```

✔ Find It

Food labels often contain health claims. Determine what type of health claim each of the following relationships would be considered. Use **A** for authorized health claim, **S** for health claims based on authoritative statements, and **Q** for qualified health claims.

_____   whole-grain cereal and the risk of heart disease

_____   folate and neural tube defects

_____   dietary fat and cancer

_____   nuts and heart disease

_____   potassium and the risk of hypertension

_____   sodium and hypertension

_____   selenium and cancer

✔ Think About It

Compare the two labels below.

Nutri-Grain Cereal Bar	**GoLean Protein and Fiber Bar**

Nutrition Facts		**Nutrition Facts**	
Serving Size 1 bar (37g)		Serving Size 1 bar (45g)	
Servings Per Container 1 bar		Servings Per Container 1 bar	
Amount Per Serving		**Amount Per Serving**	
Calories 140	Calories from Fat 25	**Calories** 170	Calories from Fat 45
	% Daily Value*		**% Daily Value***
Total Fat 3g	5%	**Total Fat** 5g	8%
Saturated Fat 0.5g	3%	Saturated Fat 2.5g	13%
Trans Fat 0g		*Trans* Fat 0g	
Cholesterol 0g	0%	**Cholesterol** 0mg	0%
Sodium 120mg	5%	**Sodium** 210mg	9%
Total Carbohydrate 26g	9%	**Total Carbohydrate** 27g	9%
Dietary Fiber <1g	3%	Dietary Fiber 5g	20%
Sugars 13g		Sugars 13g	
Protein 1g		**Protein** 8g	
Vitamin A 15% • Vitamin C 0%		Vitamin A 0% • Vitamin C 15%	
Calcium 20% • Iron 10%		Calcium 20% • Iron 10%	
* Percent Daily Values are based on a 2,000 calorie diet. Your daily values may be higher or lower depending on your calorie needs:		* Percent Daily Values are based on a 2,000 calorie diet. Your daily values may be higher or lower depending on your calorie needs:	

1. Which product contains the most calories in a single serving? _____

2. If you calculate the calories per gram for each product, how do they compare?

    _____

    _____

3. Which product has the most fat and saturated fat? _____

4. Which product has the most carbohydrate? _____ sugar? _____ fiber? _____

5. Do you think the names of these products fit? Why or why not?

    _____

    _____

6. Which product would you pick? _____

✔ Apply It

Set up your own label comparison. Select three comparable food items (such as snack crackers, cookies, frozen desserts, dairy products like yogurt, and so on). Pick items in which at least one carries a health claim. Fill in the Nutrition Facts in the blank labels provided. Identify each product.

Nutrition Facts		**Nutrition Facts**		**Nutrition Facts**	
Serving Size		Serving Size		Serving Size	
Servings Per Container		Servings Per Container		Servings Per Container	
Amount Per Serving		**Amount Per Serving**		**Amount Per Serving**	
Calories	Calories from Fat	**Calories**	Calories from Fat	**Calories**	Calories from Fat
	% Daily Value*		**% Daily Value***		**% Daily Value***
Total Fat		**Total Fat**		**Total Fat**	
Saturated Fat		Saturated Fat		Saturated Fat	
Trans Fat		*Trans* Fat		*Trans* Fat	
Cholesterol		**Cholesterol**		**Cholesterol**	
Sodium		**Sodium**		**Sodium**	
Total Carbohydrate		**Total Carbohydrate**		**Total Carbohydrate**	
Dietary Fiber		Dietary Fiber		Dietary Fiber	
Sugars		Sugars		Sugars	
Protein		**Protein**		**Protein**	
Vitamin A • Vitamin C		Vitamin A • Vitamin C		Vitamin A • Vitamin C	
Calcium • Iron • Vitamin D		Calcium • Iron • Vitamin D		Calcium • Iron • Vitamin D	
* Percent Daily Values are based on a 2,000 calorie diet. Your daily values may be higher or lower depending on your calorie needs:		* Percent Daily Values are based on a 2,000 calorie diet. Your daily values may be higher or lower depending on your calorie needs:		* Percent Daily Values are based on a 2,000 calorie diet. Your daily values may be higher or lower depending on your calorie needs:	

Product: _____   Product: _____   Product: _____

1. What have you learned by comparing the labels?

    _____

    _____

    _____

2. Which product would you choose to use yourself? Why?

    _____

    _____

    _____

✓ Test It

1. The following claim is made on a food label: "May cure the common cold." This is an example of a(n) _____ health claim.

    a. authorized

    b. authoritative statement

    c. qualified

    d. illegal

2. The Food and Drug Administration requires all of the following information on a food label except

    a. price.

    b. ingredients.

    c. contact information for the manufacturer.

    d. the calories from fat per serving.

Functional Foods: What Role Do They Play in Your Diet?

✓ Know It

Match the terms on the left with the descriptors on the right. Each descriptor may apply to more than one term.

_____ 1. health benefits

_____ 2. animal compounds

_____ 3. plant chemicals

_____ 4. treatment of chronic diseases

a. functional foods

b. phytochemicals

c. zoochemicals

✓ Find It

*Phytochemical or zoochemical? Use **P** for phytochemical or **Z** for zoochemical for each of the following functional foods.*

_____ lycopene in ketchup

_____ active-culture yogurt

_____ beta-carotene in spinach

_____ soy in tofu

_____ fish oils added to pasta

✓ Think About It

You are shopping in the campus store and notice that you can purchase potato chips with added oat bran, active-culture yogurt, and cookies with psyllium and soy. These are all examples of _____.

If you had only enough money for one of these foods, which would be the healthiest natural choice?

_____ Why would you make that choice? _____

_____

✔ Apply It

1. Look in your cupboard and refrigerator at home. What products do you presently have that could be considered functional foods?

_____

_____

2. What functional foods do you plan to purchase in the future?

_____

_____

✔ Test It

1. Functional foods include all of the following except

   a. orange juice.

   b. fortified margarine.

   c. oatmeal.

   d. low-sodium chicken noodle soup.

2. The best source of phytochemicals is

   a. fortified cereal products.

   b. fresh fruits and vegetables.

   c. nutrient supplements.

   d. foods with added plant sterols.

Two Points of View

Are Super-Sized Portions a Super Problem for Americans?

Read two professionals' opinions on this topic at the end of the chapter in your textbook, then consider the following questions:

1. Both experts agree that portion sizes in restaurant meals have increased. Some of the reasons given for this increase include choice and flexibility, good value for the money, and to increase customer loyalty. Which of these reasons do you identify as being the most influential?

    _____

    _____

2. What other reasons can you add?

    _____

    _____

3. Do you think choosing how much to eat is entirely up to a customer? Why or why not?

    _____

    _____

4. One of the experts, Barbara Rolls, states that "[They] need help from the restaurant industry." What do you think of this statement?

    _____

    _____

5. Shelia Conn, representing the restaurant industry, says that according to industry research, 71 percent of adults agreed that there are enough portion sizes available at restaurants. Do you agree with this assumption? Why or why not? What is your experience?

    _____

    _____

6. Barbara Rolls' final statement is, "The focus in restaurants should be on the quality of the food, not on the quantity." Do you agree?

_____

_____

7. Which expert do you most identify with? Why?

_____

_____

8. What can you add as a third point to these Two Points of View?

_____

_____

3 The Basics of Digestion

What Makes Eating So Enjoyable?

✔ Know It

Match each term with the appropriate description.

_____ 1. physical need for food   a. appetite

_____ 2. physical need for water   b. umami

_____ 3. psychological desire to eat or drink   c. flavor

_____ 4. taste and aroma   d. hunger

_____ 5. Japanese for delicious   e. thirst

✔ Find It

Where on your tongue would you taste each of these foods?

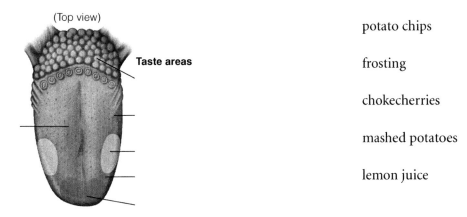

(Top view)

Taste areas

potato chips

frosting

chokecherries

mashed potatoes

lemon juice

(Refer to page 63 in your textbook for a full-color version of this image.)

✔ Think About It

1. You woke up late and don't want to miss your class. You grab an apple to satisfy your _____.

2. Walking by the coffee cart with steaming fresh caramel rolls is likely to trigger your _____.

3. Participating in a midmorning aerobics class is likely to leave you feeling the need to quench your

_____.

✔ Apply It

1. What are your favorite foods?

_____

_____

2. Do you tend to like sweet, salty, sour, or bitter tastes?

_____

_____

3. If you had to pick one meal that is umami, what would it be?

_____

_____

✔ Test It

1. Appetite can be affected by
   a. the aroma of food.
   b. the sight of food.
   c. foods you like.
   d. all of the above.

2. The five basic categories of taste include sweet, sour, bitter, savory, and
   a. umami.
   b. spicy.
   c. salty.
   d. bland.

What Is Digestion and Why Is It Important?

✔ Know It

Match each term with the appropriate description.

_____ 1. organs of the digestive tract	a. peristalsis
_____ 2. breakdown of food to be absorbed	b. chemical digestion
_____ 3. breaking down food by chewing	c. gastrointestinal tract
_____ 4. breaking down food through chemical reactions	d. mechanical digestion
_____ 5. rhythmic motion of the digestive tract	e. digestive process

✔ Find It

Put these terms under the correct category.

chew   grind   digestive juices   enzymes   mouth   stomach

absorbable nutrients

Mechanical Digestion	Chemical Digestion

✔ Think About It

While hurrying through the café, you swallow a large bite of sandwich. It feels as though it is stuck halfway down to your stomach. What step of the digestive process did you attempt to bypass?

_____

✔ Apply It

1. What foods do you like that take a great deal of mechanical digestion?

_____

_____

2. Do you think the taste of that food changes the longer it is in your mouth? Why or why not?

_____

_____

✔ Test It

1. Peristalsis is
    a. a form of mechanical digestion.
    b. forward, rhythmic motion.
    c. a form of chemical digestion.
    d. both a and b.
    e. all of the above.

2. The start of the gastrointestinal tract is the
    a. mouth.
    b. stomach.
    c. esophagus.
    d. pancreas.
    e. small intestine.

What Happens in the Individual Organs of the GI Tract?

✔ Know It

Match each term with the appropriate description.

_____	1. most digestion and absorption occurs here	a. mouth
_____	2. where food mixes with enzymes	b. esophagus
_____	3. water and electrolytes can be absorbed here	c. stomach
_____	4. digestion begins here	d. small intestine
_____	5. where the bolus travels from mouth to stomach	e. large intestine

✔ Know It, Too

Match each term with the appropriate description.

_____ 1. watery fluid of the mouth   a. pepsin

_____ 2. viscous, slippery solution   b. chyme

_____ 3. chewed mass of food   c. gastrin

_____ 4. liquid combination of products of digestion   d. mucus

_____ 5. protein digestive enzyme   e. saliva

_____ 6. stomach digestive hormone   f. feces

_____ 7. waste products   g. bolus

✔ Find It

Fill in the spelling of each term described. Put the each letter in an "O" into the phrase below. What terms where described?

D ◯ ◯ ◯ ◯ T ◯ ◯ E   ◯ E ◯ ◯ E T ◯ ◯ S

__ ◯ __ __   stored in the gallbladder

◯ __ __ __ __ __ __   one of the stomach secretions

◯ __ __ __ __ __ ◯   chemicals that break down food

__ __ __ ◯◯ __   moistens food in the mouth

__ __ __ __ ◯   acts as a lubricant

__ __ __ __ __ ◯ __ __ __ ◯ __ __   stomach acid

__ ◯ __ __ __ ◯◯ __ __ __   neutralizes stomach acid

✔ Think About It

1. You dash to your apartment for lunch and see that you have a choice of ramen noodles, macaroni and cheese, or a jelly sandwich on white bread. You won't have a chance to eat again for at least three hours. Which lunch would have the most satiety?

   _____

2. Your choice of a beverage with that lunch is water, diet soda, orange juice, or low-fat milk. Which would help the lunch to have the most satiety? _____

✔ Apply It

1. What is a typical breakfast for you?

   _____

   _____

2. Do you feel that you are hungry again in less than two hours? Why?

   _____

   _____

3. What could you add to your breakfast to make it ward off hunger sensations longer?

   _____

   _____

✔ Test It

1. Most digestion and absorption occurs in the

   a. stomach.

   b. small intestine.

   c. large intestine.

   d. liver.

2. The large intestine can

   a. get rid of body waste in the form of feces.

   b. absorb a majority of the nutrients not absorbed in the small intestine.

   c. contribute to the digestion of protein.

   d. produce hormones needed by the body for digestion.

What Other Body Systems Affect Your Use of Nutrients?

✔ Know It

Match the body system with its primary function(s).

_____	1. contains white blood cells; fluid transportation	a.	nervous system
_____	2. eliminates waste products from the circulatory system	b.	circulatory system
_____	3. communicates when to eat, drink, and stop	c.	lymphatic system
_____	4. primary transportation system	d.	excretory system

✔ Find It

Arrange these terms and phrases under the appropriate body system.

network of capillaries   hormones   waste products   hunger sensation

carries oxygen and nutrients   stop eating   removes carbon dioxide

fat-soluble vitamins   urine   heart and lungs   immune system

Nervous System	Circulatory System
Lymphatic System	**Excretory System**

✔ Think About It

You ended up having to work a double shift. To stay awake, you drank 3 cups of coffee. As the second shift ends, you feel dizzy and weak. Which body system is giving you this message?

_____

✔ Apply It

1. How do you know when your excretory system is working well?

_____

2. What can you do to speed up the production of urine?

_____

✔ Test It

1. Carbon dioxide is removed from the blood in the

   a. small intestine.

   b. heart.

   c. lungs.

   d. kidneys.

2. Waste products excreted through the urine are concentrated in the

   a. large intestine.

   b. heart.

   c. blood.

   d. kidneys.

What Are Some Common Digestive Disorders?

✔ Know It

Match the digestive disorder with the body site where it occurs.

	Digestive Disorder		**Body Site**
_____	1. gingivitis	a.	mouth
_____	2. GERD	b.	esophagus
_____	3. peptic ulcer	c.	stomach
_____	4. periodontal disease	d.	gallbladder
_____	5. constipation	e.	intestines
_____	6. heartburn		
_____	7. irritable bowel syndrome		
_____	8. gastroenteritis		
_____	9. dysphagia		
_____	10. diarrhea		

✔ Find It

What terms are being defined? Insert them in the correct spaces, across or down.

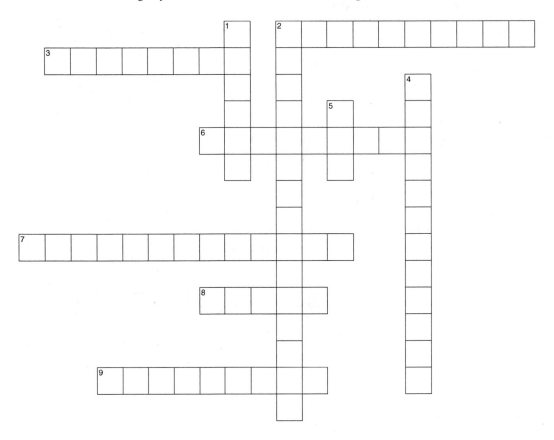

Across

2 crystallization of compounds in the gallbladder
3 frequent, loose, watery stools
6 reflux of gastric juice
7 inflammation of the gums
8 sore in mucosal lining of stomach
9 difficulty swallowing

Down

1 abnormally growing cells
2 stomach flu
4 difficulty passing stools
5 irritable bowel syndrome

✔ Think About It

After eating a large steak dinner complete with sour cream mashed potatoes, tossed salad, white roll, and a glass of wine, then smoking a postmeal cigarette, you begin to feel a burning sensation in your chest. Most likely, you are experiencing the common digestive disorder known as _____.

To help yourself feel better, you should _____.

So that you don't experience these symptoms again, you should _____

_____.

✔ Apply It

1. What are your typical eating habits?

   _____

   _____

2. How often do you eat during a typical day?

   _____

   _____

3. How large are your meals?

   _____

   _____

4. Do you have any digestion-related problems?

   _____

   _____

5. Can you list any treatments that could help your digestion?

   _____

   _____

✓ Test It

1. Irritable bowel syndrome

    a. causes tissue damage to the colon.

    b. is a functional disorder of the colon rhythm.

    c. can only be managed by using prescription drugs.

    d. generally causes little discomfort.

2. Celiac disease

    a. is an illness of the large intestine.

    b. is more common among African Americans.

    c. is the inability to digest the protein in gluten.

    d. is treated with a low-fat diet.

Two Points of View

How Effective Is the Weight-Loss Drug Orlistat?

The weight-loss drug orlistat (Xenical) is currently a prescription drug. It may soon become an over-the-counter drug. Read two professionals' opinions on this topic at the end of the chapter in your textbook, then consider the following questions:

1. How does this drug work?

    _____

    _____

2. What are possible side effects of the drug?

    _____

    _____

3. Do you think the average consumer will use this drug appropriately? Why or why not?

    _____

    _____

4. Which expert's advice, that of James Anderson, MD, or Madelyn Fernstrom, PhD, CNS, would you be most likely to listen to? Why?

_____

_____

5. Would you consider using this drug if you needed to lose weight? Why or why not?

_____

_____

6. Would you recommend this product to a friend? Why or why not?

_____

_____

4
Carbohydrates
Sugars, Starches, and Fiber

What Are Carbohydrates and Why Do You Need Them?

✔ Know It

Match the plant-based carbohydrate with the region where it is predominantly used.

_____ 1. rice

_____ 2. bananas, chilies, beans, tubers

_____ 3. pasta, bread, couscous

_____ 4. potato, bread

a. Latin America

b. United States

c. Asia

✔ Find It

Check each food that provides a good source of carbohydrate.

_____ apples and oranges

_____ hamburger steak

_____ low-fat milk

_____ squash and sweet potato

_____ garbanzo beans

_____ mozzarella cheese

_____ granola

✔ Think About It

You get up late and skip breakfast in a rush to get to class. By doing this, you have neglected to feed your

_____ and _____.

✔ Apply It

1. Write down what you had for breakfast today.

_____

_____

_____

2. Circle the foods that were the primary sources of carbohydrate.

3. Did you feed your brain this morning? _____

4. Do you need to make changes for tomorrow? Why or why not?

_____

_____

_____

_____

✔ Test It

1. Select the most nutrient-dense carbohydrate snack.

    a. peach smoothie made with low-fat milk

    b. grilled cheese sandwich and soda pop

    c. caramel popcorn and Kool-Aid

    d. pretzels and beer

2. Good sources of both carbohydrate and protein include

    a. cheese, sour cream, and eggs.

    b. bread, cereal, and rice.

    c. potato, broccoli, and raisins.

    d. nuts, legumes, and soybeans.

What Are Simple and Complex Carbohydrates?

✓ Know It

Fill in this crossword puzzle using carbohydrate terms.

Across

2   storage form of carbohydrate in plants
5   multiple single units
7   primary fuel supply
8   monosaccharide in fruit
9   glucose + fructose
10 monosaccharide in milk
11 nondigestible polysaccharide
12 single sugar

Down

1   glucose + glucose
3   storage form of carbohydrate in humans
4   glucose + galactose
6   two sugar units

✔ Find It

Fill in the missing blanks for the simple carbohydrates.

Monosaccharides

_____ _____ Galactose

Disaccharides

Sucrose   Maltose   _____

(Refer to page 90 in your textbook for a full-color version of this image.)

✔ Find More

*Label each of the following fiber sources as soluble (**S**) or insoluble (**I**).*

_____ oats

_____ bran flakes

_____ seeds in fruits and vegetables

_____ pectin in fruit

_____ gums in legumes

_____ beans

✔ Think About It

1. Your roommate made lunch for you. It consists of a grilled cheese sandwich (white bread and processed cheese food), potato chips, and a fruit drink. What could you add to this lunch to increase the fiber content?

    _____

2. It's your turn to make lunch tomorrow, and you're still concerned with increasing fiber in your diet. What will your menu be?

    _____

    _____

✓ Apply It

Go to the breakfast cereal aisle at the grocery store. Fill in the labels below using the information from three different products. Identify the products in the spaces below each Nutrition Facts label.

Nutrition Facts	**Nutrition Facts**	**Nutrition Facts**
Serving Size Servings Per Container	Serving Size Servings Per Container	Serving Size Servings Per Container
Amount Per Serving	**Amount Per Serving**	**Amount Per Serving**
Calories Calories from Fat	**Calories** Calories from Fat	**Calories** Calories from Fat
% Daily Value*	% Daily Value*	% Daily Value*
Total Fat	**Total Fat**	**Total Fat**
Saturated Fat	Saturated Fat	Saturated Fat
Trans Fat	*Trans* Fat	*Trans* Fat
Cholesterol	**Cholesterol**	**Cholesterol**
Sodium	**Sodium**	**Sodium**
Total Carbohydrate	**Total Carbohydrate**	**Total Carbohydrate**
Dietary Fiber	Dietary Fiber	Dietary Fiber
Sugars	Sugars	Sugars
Protein	**Protein**	**Protein**
Vitamin A • Vitamin C	Vitamin A • Vitamin C	Vitamin A • Vitamin C
Calcium • Iron • Vitamin D	Calcium • Iron • Vitamin D	Calcium • Iron • Vitamin D
* Percent Daily Values are based on a 2,000 calorie diet. Your daily values may be higher or lower depending on your calorie needs:	* Percent Daily Values are based on a 2,000 calorie diet. Your daily values may be higher or lower depending on your calorie needs:	* Percent Daily Values are based on a 2,000 calorie diet. Your daily values may be higher or lower depending on your calorie needs:

Product:

_____

Product:

_____

Product:

_____

1. How does the total carbohydrate per serving compare among these products?

    _____

2. Which product has the most simple carbohydrate (sugar)?

    _____

3. Which product has the highest amount of fiber per serving?

    _____

4. Which product would you choose to eat? Why?

    _____

✔ Test It

1. The disaccharides include

   a. glucose, sucrose, galactose.

   b. maltose, lactose, sucrose.

   c. galactose, sucrose, maltose.

   d. glucose, fructose, galactose.

2. The storage form of carbohydrate in the body is termed

   a. photosynthesis.

   b. starch.

   c. glycogen.

   d. functional fiber.

Grains, Glorious Whole Grains

✔ Know It

Match each term to the appropriate description.

_____ 1. indigestible shell of a grain kernel   a. whole grains

_____ 2. seed of the grain kernel   b. endosperm

_____ 3. starch part of the grain kernel   c. enriched grains

_____ 4. grain food that excludes the bran and germ   d. bran

_____ 5. grain foods made with the entire kernel   e. refined grain

_____ 6. refined grains with nutrients added   f. germ

✔ Find It

1. Label the bran, germ, and endosperm on the diagram of the grain kernel.

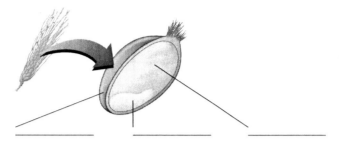

(Refer to page 93 in your textbook for a full-color version of this image.)

2. List these nutrients under the appropriate parts of the grain above: high fiber, unsaturated fat, starch, protein, B vitamins, vitamin E.

✔ Think About It

1. While you are at home over the weekend, you watch your grandmother make bread. She uses a couple of kinds of flour, including cracked wheat and bleached white flour. What can you tell her about the nutrient content of these flours?

_____

_____

_____

2. Why does your grandmother use both of these flours in the bread?

_____

_____

_____

✓ Apply It

How often do you have each of the following whole-grain products? Fill in the chart.

Food Item	2–3 Times per Week	Once a Week	Once a Month	Never
Popcorn				
Brown rice				
Oatmeal				
Whole-wheat bread				
Barley				
Other				

1.   What have you learned about your intake of whole-grain products?

_____

2.   Do you need to make any changes? _____

3.   If so, what should you change? _____

✓ Test It

1.   Enriched grain products

    a.   include the bran and germ.

    b.   include the entire edible grain kernel.

    c.   include the seed.

    d.   have B vitamins added.

2.   Whole-grain products may

    a.   increase the risk of diabetes.

    b.   contribute to strokes.

    c.   reduce the risk of heart disease.

    d.   cause some forms of cancer.

What Happens to the Carbohydrate You Eat?

✔ Know It

Fill in the letter blanks for the organs described below. Put the letter in each circle into the headline term. What do the terms describe?

◯◯ G ◯◯◯◯◯ N

___ ___ ___ ___ ◯   monosaccharides travel through the body

___ ◯ ___ ◯ ___   monosaccharides are converted to glucose here

◯◯ ___ ___ ___ ___ ___   acids added and amylase deactivated

◯ ___ ___ ___ ___ ___ ___ ___   disaccharides broken down to monosaccharides

___ ◯ ___ ___ ___   carbohydrate digestion begins here

✔ Find It

Number the order of the steps from 1 to 6 in the carbohydrate-digestion process.

_____   Starch breaks down to disaccharides.

_____   Fiber leaves the body.

_____   Disaccharides break down to monosaccharides.

_____   Starch breaks down into smaller units.

_____   Glucose is distributed throughout the body.

_____   Monosaccharides are converted to glucose.

✔ Think About It

1. Your friend avoids drinking milk. He says that milk causes him to feel bloated and to have frequent diarrhea. Most likely your friend has _____.

2. The enzyme that he lacks to digest dairy products is _____.

3. What dairy products might your friend be able to tolerate? _____

✔ Apply It

How much lactose is in the food you eat? Estimate your lactose intake for one day.

Table 4.1

How Much Lactose Is in Your Foods?

Food	Amount	Lactose (grams)
Milk, whole, 1%, or skim	1 cup	11
Lactaid milk	1 cup	<1
Soy milk	1 cup	0
Ice cream	½ cup	6
Yogurt, low fat	1 cup	5
Sherbet	½ cup	2
Cottage cheese	½ cup	2
Swiss, Blue, Cheddar, Parmesan cheese	1 oz	1
Cream cheese	1 oz	1

1. Have you ever had symptoms of lactose intolerance? _____

2. If so, what can you do? _____

✓ Test It

1. Lactose intolerance is
    a. an allergy to milk.
    b. the immune system's response to protein.
    c. lack of the lactase enzyme.
    d. a serious medical condition.

2. Sucrose is broken down to fructose and glucose in the
    a. mouth.
    b. stomach.
    c. small intestine.
    d. liver.

How Does Your Body Use Carbohydrates?

✓ Know It

Match the definition to the appropriate word fragment.

_____ 1. glyco

_____ 2. genesis

_____ 3. neo

_____ 4. lysis

a. new

b. loosening, breaking down

c. origin, the beginning of

d. sweet, sugar

Using the definitions from above, identify what each word means.

1. glycogenesis _____ _____

2. glycogenolysis _____ _____

3. gluconeogenesis _____ _____ _____

✔ Find It

Where in the body does each process occur? Match the organ or body part with the corresponding process. (Each organ or body part may be used more than once, and each process may occur in more than one organ or body part.)

_____ 1. glycogenesis   a. muscle

_____ 2. gluconeogenesis   b. liver

_____ 3. release of glycogen   c. body fat

_____ 4. store excess glycogen   d. pancreas

_____ 5. release of insulin

_____ 6. ketone bodies

✔ Think About It

1. For many days prior to a competition, bodybuilders strictly fast, taking in only water. What are the possible consequences of this fasting technique?

    _____

2. What would you tell a friend who is thinking of fasting? _____

    _____

✔ Apply It

1. Describe the process that occurs when you skip breakfast.

    _____

    _____

2. Do you routinely skip breakfast? _____

3. If so, do you think you should make any changes? _____

4. If not, why not? _____

✓ Test It

1. Glycogen can be stored in all of the following body locations except the
   a. pancreas.
   b. liver.
   c. muscle.
   d. body fat.

2. When blood glucose levels drop, the pancreas releases
   a. insulin.
   b. glucagon.
   c. glycogen.
   d. ketone bodies.

How Much Carbohydrate Do You Need and What Are Its Food Sources?

✓ Know It

*What type of carbohydrates are found in each food group? Use **S** for simple and **C** for complex to note the type of carbohydrate in each of the following foods.*

_____   fresh fruit

_____   whole grains

_____   dairy foods

_____   legumes and beans

_____   vegetables

_____   sugar, sweets

Looking at the list above, circle each food group that has fiber.

✔ Find It

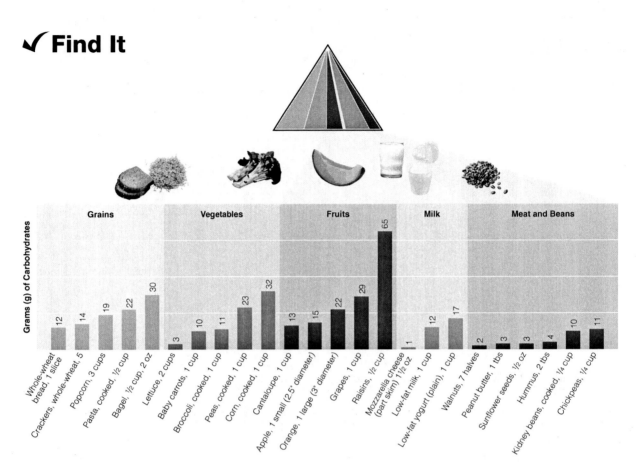

(Refer to page 100 in your textbook for a full-color version of this image.)

Finish this chart by filling in the empty spaces using information from the figure above.

Food Item	Food Item	Food Item	Total Carbohydrate
2 slices whole-wheat bread 24 g		1 apple 16 g	44 g
	1½ ounces cheese 1 g	½ cup milk 6 g	51 g
3 cups popcorn 19 g		½ ounce sunflower seeds 5 g	89 g
1 cup broccoli 11 g		1 cup carrots 10 g	
1 bagel 60 g	2 tablespoons peanut butter 4 g		96 g

✔ Think About It

The following menu was posted on the Mess Hall door at the summer camp where you are planning to be a camp counselor.

Breakfast
Assorted Cold Cereals
Toast
Butter, Jelly
Orange Drink
Coffee

Lunch
Grilled Cheese Sandwich
Potato Chips
Fruit Cocktail
Milk

Dinner
Hobo Stew
Crackers
Ice Cream Sundaes

1. Does this menu look like a nutrient-dense diet for active young people? _____

2. What else would you like to know about the menu ingredients?

   _____

   _____

3. What suggestions do you have for the cook?

   _____

   _____

✔ Apply It

1. Go to a vending area of your school. List what is commonly available in the vending machines.

   _____

   _____

2. Are there any options available that are nutrient dense and low in saturated fat? If so, list them.

   _____

3. If not, suggest how these machines could be changed.

   _____

   _____

✔ Test It

1. According to the DRIs, a 2,000-calorie meal plan should include _____ grams of fiber.

    a. 7

    b. 14

    c. 28

    d. 32

2. Good sources of complex carbohydrates occur naturally in

    a. oranges, bread, and kidney beans.

    b. popcorn, walnuts, and yogurt.

    c. beef jerky, sunflower seeds, and beer.

    d. fruit-flavored drinks, canned fruit, and ice cream.

What's the Difference Between Natural and Added Sugars?

✔ Know It

Sugar is often added to processed foods. Which of these are possible reasons why sugar is added to a food item?

Check all that apply.

_____ keep cookies moist

_____ add to the structure of a dessert bar

_____ add calories

_____ help a pie crust to brown when baked

_____ act as a preservative

_____ thicken a sauce

_____ add unsaturated fat

_____ add flavor

_____ increase energy

✔ Find It

Listed below is the information from two food labels. Circle all of the ingredients that are a form of sugar.

Label 1

Nutrition Facts: 80 Calories (25 g) per serving, 0 g Total Fat, 19 g Total Carbohydrate, 0 g Fiber, 13 g Sugar, 1 g Protein

Ingredients: corn syrup, apple puree concentrate, water, modified corn starch, gelatin, contains two percent or less of citric acid (vitamin C), natural and artificial flavor, color added, hydrogenated coconut oil.

Label 2

Nutrition Facts: 90 Calories (24 g) per serving, 2 g Total Fat, 19 g Total Carbohydrate, 1 g Fiber, 7 g Sugar, 1 g Protein

Ingredients: whole-grain rolled oats, sugar, rice flour, whole-grain rolled wheat, partially hydrogenated soybean and cottonseed oils, whole-wheat flour, molasses, sodium bicarbonate, soy lecithin, caramel color, barley malt, salt, nonfat dry milk, corn syrup, crisp rice (rice, sugar, salt, barley malt), semi-sweet chocolate chunks (sugar, chocolate liquor, cocoa butter, vanilla), sugar, corn syrup solids, glycerin, high-fructose corn syrup, sorbitol, fructose, calcium carbonate, natural and artificial flavors, salt, molasses, water, citric acid.

✔ Think About It

1. Look at the information from Labels 1 and 2 above. What are the major similarities between the Nutrition Facts of Label 1 and Label 2?

    _____

    _____

2. What are the major differences between them?

    _____

3. Which product do you think is Kellogg's fruit-flavored snack? Why?

_____

4. Which product do you think is Quaker Chewy Chocolate Chunk Granola Bar? Why?

_____

5. Which would you choose as the "better" snack? Why?

_____

_____

✔ Apply It

Investigate the foods in your cupboard to determine how much added sugar there is in foods you commonly have on hand. Choose at least five food labels to analyze.

Product Name	Total Carbohydrate g	Sugar g	Calories from Carbohydrate	Percent of Carbohydrate from Sugar
Example: Chips Ahoy Cookies	22 g	11 g	88 calories	50%

1. What did you learn about common products in your cupboard?

_____

_____

2. Do you plan to make any purchasing changes? If so, what will they be?

_____

_____

_____

3. If not, why not?

_____

_____

_____

✔ Test It

1. Added sugars in a diet can
   a. cause hyperactivity in children.
   b. cause diabetes.
   c. cause excessive weight gain.
   d. increase blood triglycerides.

2. The number-one way that many Americans consume too much added sugar is in the form of
   a. breakfast cereal products.
   b. snack-type cookie products.
   c. beverages.
   d. fresh fruits.

What Are Sugar Substitutes and What Forms Can They Take?

✓ Know It

Match the sugar substitute to the appropriate description.

_____	1.	polyol used in sugarless chewing gum and candy; excess may cause diarrhea	a.	sucralose
_____	2.	polyol as sweet as sucrose; also used in pharmaceutical and hygiene products	b.	saccharin
_____	3.	Sweet 'N Low; can be used in baking	c.	acesulfame-K
_____	4.	Nutrasweet or Equal; breaks down to amino acids	d.	sorbitol or mannitol
_____	5.	Splenda; table-top sweetener; not absorbed by the body	e.	neotame
_____	6.	Sunette; 200 times sweeter than sucrose; not metabolized by the body	f.	xylitol
_____	7.	aspartic acid + phenylalanine; eliminated in the urine and stool	g.	aspartame

✓ Find It

In what foods are sugar substitutes used? Check all of the possible foods in which manufacturers may use a sugar substitute.

_____ chewing gum and candy

_____ baked goods

_____ potato chips and pretzels

_____ toothpaste

_____ vitamin supplements

_____ snack crackers

_____ beverages

✔ Think About It

You are at home for a family reunion. Your aunt, knowing that you are taking a nutrition course, proceeds to tell you about her experiences with aspartame. She says that she gets headaches whenever she drinks a product that contains it and that she had read on the Internet that it could cause someone to develop PKU. What advice can you give to your aunt?

_____

_____

_____

✔ Apply It

Visit a grocery store and try to find at least one food or pharmaceutical item that has each of the following sweeteners added.

Sugar Substitute	Food Item or Pharmaceutical Product
sorbitol	
mannitol	
xylitol	
saccharin	
aspartame	
sucralose	

1. Which one surprised you? _____

2. Why was the sugar substitute used in that particular product? _____

_____

✔ Test It

1. Possible side effects of sugar alcohols include
   a. increased risk of bladder cancer.
   b. diarrhea.
   c. dental caries.
   d. diabetes.

2. The majority of aspartame consumed in the United States is in
   a. gums and candies.
   b. frozen desserts.
   c. soft drinks.
   d. pharmaceuticals (including toothpaste).

Why Is Fiber so Important?

✔ Know It

Match the term with the appropriate definition.

_____	1. pectin, gums; found in citrus fruits, oats, carrots	a. diverticula
_____	2. disorder often caused by long-term constipation	b. soluble fiber
_____	3. bulges or weak spots in the colon	c. insoluble fiber
_____	4. inflammation or infection of diverticula	d. diverticulosis
_____	5. cellulose, hemicellulose; found in whole grains	e. diverticulitis

✔ Find It

Fiber is thought to reduce the risk of many chronic health conditions. Fill in the blanks with the chronic illness from the list below that the described action of fiber may help to reduce. Some terms will be used more than once.

heart disease   diabetes   cancer   obesity

_____   1.   High-fiber foods can lead to satiation.

_____   2.   Viscous, soluble fibers help lower elevated blood cholesterol levels.

_____   3.   Viscous, soluble fibers may reduce the rate at which fat and carbohydrate are absorbed.

_____   4.   Fiber can slow down digestion and absorption of glucose.

_____   5.   Fiber encourages the growth of friendly bacteria in the colon.

✔ Think About It

You open the bathroom cabinet and notice that your roommate has purchased a supplement that contains psyllium. When you ask your roommate about it, she says that she has occasional constipation and another friend told her to use that product. What could you recommend to your roommate?

_____

_____

_____

_____

✔ Apply It

Go to the grocery store and compare the fiber content listed on the Nutrition Facts of three similar products (for example, three different breads or three different cereals).

Product Name	Total Carbohydrate g	Sugar g	Fiber g

1. What did you learn about these products?

   _____

   _____

2. Does having more fiber mean that there is more total carbohydrate?

   _____

   _____

✔ Test It

1. All of the following foods contain good sources of fiber except
   a. oatmeal with raisins.
   b. whole-grain crackers and hummus.
   c. sardines with bones.
   d. green beans with walnuts.

2. Insoluble fiber
   a. dissolves in water.
   b. includes psyllium and pectin.
   c. is found in whole grains, oats, and fruits.
   d. increases the risk of constipation.

What Is Diabetes Mellitus and Why Is It an Epidemic?

✓ Know It

Match each term with the appropriate definition.

_____	1. most prevalent form of diabetes	a. insulin resistance
_____	2. type of diabetes generally seen in children	b. insulin
_____	3. cells do not respond to insulin	c. prediabetes
_____	4. lack of insulin leading to ketone bodies	d. type 1
_____	5. impaired glucose tolerance	e. type 2
_____	6. hormone needed for glucose to enter a cell	f. ketoacidosis

✓ Find It

List each diabetes treatment option under the appropriate diabetes diagnosis.

weight reduction   balanced diet   self-glucose monitoring   insulin therapy

medication   exercise

Prediabetes	Type 1 Diabetes	Type 2 Diabetes

✔ Think About It

1. You are working in an after-school program for elementary students. The school is worried about the increased incidence of type 2 diabetes in children nationwide. What might you observe in these children that could put them at risk of this chronic illness?

   _____

   _____

   _____

   _____

2. What could you do to help with this issue?

   _____

   _____

   _____

   _____

 **Apply It**

Are You at Risk for Type 2 Diabetes?

Take the following quiz to assess if you are at a higher risk for developing type 2 diabetes. Whereas this list contains the presently known risk factors for type 2 diabetes, there may be others. If you have questions or doubts, check with your doctor.

Do you have a body mass index (BMI) of 25 or higher*? **Yes** ☐ **No** ☐

If you answered no, you don't need to continue. If you answered yes, continue.

1. Does your mom, dad, brother, or sister have diabetes? **Yes** ☐ **No** ☐
2. Do you typically get little exercise? **Yes** ☐ **No** ☐
3. Are you of African-American, Alaska Native, Native American, Asian-American, Hispanic-American, or Pacific Islander-American descent? **Yes** ☐ **No** ☐
4. Have you ever delivered a baby that weighed more than 9 pounds at birth? **Yes** ☐ **No** ☐
5. Have you ever had diabetes during pregnancy? **Yes** ☐ **No** ☐
6. Do you have a blood pressure of 140/90 millimeters of mercury (mmHg) or higher? **Yes** ☐ **No** ☐
7. Have you been told by your doctor that you have too much fatty triglycerides (fat) in your blood (more than 250 mg/dl) or too little of the "good" HDL cholesterol (less than 35 mg/dl)? **Yes** ☐ **No** ☐
8. Have you ever had blood glucose test results that were higher than normal? **Yes** ☐ **No** ☐
9. Have you ever been told that you have vascular disease or problems with your blood vessels? **Yes** ☐ **No** ☐
10. Do you have polycystic ovary syndrome[†]? **Yes** ☐ **No** ☐

Answers

If you are overweight and answered yes to any of the above questions, you could benefit from speaking with your doctor.

*BMI is a measure of your weight in relationship to your height. See Chapter 10 for a chart to determine your BMI.

[†]Polycystic ovary syndrome is a disorder in women due to an abnormal level of hormones, including insulin. This disorder increases your risk of diabetes as well as heart disease and high blood pressure.

1. What have you learned about yourself by completing this self-assessment? _____

_____

2. Do you have any risk factors for the development of diabetes? _____

3. If one of your parents filled this in, do you think he or she would have any of these risk factors?

_____

✓ Test It

1. Diabetes is not a risk factor for

   c. colon cancer.

   b. heart disease.

   c. nerve damage.

   d. loss of eyesight.

2. A person with diabetes has a fasting blood sugar of

   a. <100 mg/dl.

   b. 100–125 mg/dl.

   c. >126 mg/dl.

   d. 200–300 mg/dl.

What Is Hypoglycemia?

✓ Know It

Match the term to the appropriate definition.

_____	1. fasting blood glucose >126 mg/dl	a. reactive hypoglycemia
_____	2. blood glucose level <70 mg/dl	b. fasting hypoglycemia
_____	3. hormone-related shakiness, dizziness, hunger hours after eating	c. hyperglycemia
_____	4. low blood glucose related to long stretches without food	d. hypoglycemia

✓ Think About It

A friend was reading a health article in a magazine and is now convinced that she has a serious medical condition called hypoglycemia. She called the student health services but cannot get an appointment for at least two days. What can you suggest that she do to treat her symptoms of shakiness and hunger?

_____

_____

✓ Apply It

1. Have you ever experienced any of the symptoms of hypoglycemia (shakiness, dizziness, hunger, or sweating)? _____

2. Can you tribute these symptoms to the last time you ate or drank something? _____

3. If so, what can you do to avoid this transient feeling in the future?

_____

✓ Test It

1. The primary treatment of hypoglycemia is
   a. insulin therapy.
   b. small, balanced meals throughout the day.
   c. a low-carbohydrate diet.
   d. restriction of activity and exercise.

2. Hypoglycemia can occur
   a. in diabetics who eat too much.
   b. when there is insufficient insulin produced by the pancreas.
   c. when someone goes without nourishment for a long time.
   d. as a result of drinking beverages with high-fructose corn syrup.

Two Points of View

Can Soft Drinks Be Part of a Healthy Diet?

Read two professionals' opinions on this topic at the end of the chapter in your textbook, then consider the following questions:

1. According to the experts in Two Points of View, how have beverages affected the health of Americans?

_____

_____

2. In answer to the question, "How can soft drinks be part of a healthy diet?" what is Robert Earl's opinion?

   _____

   _____

3. In answer to the same question, what is Barry Popkin's opinion?

   _____

   _____

4. Do you think soft drinks can be part of a healthy diet?

   _____

5. Do you drink soft drinks now? _____

6. Do you plan to change your consumption pattern? If so, how?

   _____

   _____

Fats, Oils, and Other Lipids

What Are Lipids and Why Do You Need Them?

✓ Know It

Fill in the crossword puzzle using lipid terms.

Across

1 fatty acid with two or more double bonds
4 class of lipid that includes cholesterol
6 fatty acid with all carbon bound by hydrogen
9 must be included in the diet
10 lipids that are liquid at room temperature
11 two fatty acids + phosphorus
12 fatty acid with one double bond

Down

2 organic compounds that are insoluble in water
3 fatty acid with double bonds
5 three-carbon backbone of a triglyceride
7 holds water and oil in solution
8 aversion to water

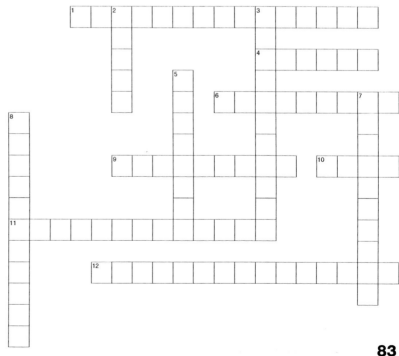

✓ Find It

Fill in the blanks using the following words or phrases:

>   satiety   transport proteins   triglyceride   insulation   sterol
>
>   aroma and flavor   phospholipid   energy storage   flaky texture
>
>   tender meats

1. The three types of lipids are _____, _____, and _____.

2. Lipids are used in cooking and food preparation for _____, _____,
    _____, and _____.

3. Lipids are essential in the body for _____, _____, and _____.

✓ Think About It

A friend of yours has joined a company that sells nutritional supplements. According to information from your friend, one of the best-selling products is lecithin, "an important nutrient needed by all cells in the body." Because you generally follow a low-fat diet, your friend is trying to convince you that you need this product.

1. What do you think?

    _____

2. What can you tell your friend about lecithin?

    _____

✓ Apply It

Complete the chart to include the number of double bonds in each type of lipid and whether or not the lipid is generally solid or liquid at room temperature.

Lipid	Number of Double Bonds	Solid or Liquid
saturated		
monounsaturated		
polyunsaturated		
linoleic acid		

✓ Test It

1. Fatty acids differ from each other in all of the following except
    a. length of carbons in the chain.
    b. number of double bonds.
    c. single or double bonds between carbon atoms.
    d. calories.

2. Phospholipids are made up of
    a. glycerol, two fatty acids, and phosphorus.
    b. essential fatty acids and potassium.
    c. polyunsaturated fatty acids and an emulsifier.
    d. triglycerides and cholesterol.

What Happens to the Fat You Eat?

✓ Know It

Fill in the letter blanks for each term described, then transfer the numbered letters to the title below to answer the question: Where does most fat digestion occur?

___ ___ ___ ___ ___ ___ ___   ___ ___ ___   ___ ___ ___ ___ ___   ___ ___ ___ ___ ___ ___ ___ ___ ___
11 10 7 5 12 4 9   12 8 6   11 5 12 2 2   1 8 10 3 11 10 1 8 3

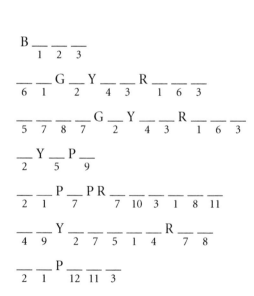

B ___ ___ ___   secretion that emulsifies fat
  1 2 3

___ ___ G ___ Y ___ ___ R ___ ___ ___   glycerol with two fatty acids
6 1   2   4 3   1 6 3

___ ___ ___ ___ G ___ Y ___ ___ R ___ ___ ___   glycerol with one fatty acid
5 7 8 7   2   4 3   1 6 3

___ Y ___ P ___   watery body fluid that carries fatty acids
2   5   9

___ ___ P ___ P R ___ ___ ___ ___ ___ ___   transport carriers for fat through body fluids
2 1 7   7 10 3 1 8 11

___ ___ Y ___ ___ ___ ___ ___ R ___ ___   large lipoprotein that carries digested fat
4 9   2 7 5 1 4   7 8

___ ___ P ___ ___ ___   enzyme that breaks down fat in the stomach
2 1 12 11 3

✔ Find It

Put the following steps of fat digestion in order from 1 to 5.

_____   Digestion continues with the aid of gastric lipase.

_____   Short-chain fatty acids enter the bloodstream.

_____   Bile acid is secreted to emulsify fat.

_____   Mechanical breakdown of food occurs.

_____   Long-chain fatty acids are reformulated to chylomicrons.

✔ Think About It

Your mother has been diagnosed with gallbladder disease. What foods do you think she was told to avoid and why?

_____

_____

✔ Apply It

Complete this chart of the lipoproteins.

Lipoprotein	Triglyceride %	Phospholipid %	Cholesterol %	Protein %	Function
chylomicron	90		5	2	
VLDL	60		12		delivers fat made in the liver to the tissues
LDL	10	15		25	
HDL		25	20	50	removes cholesterol from cells

✔ Test It

1. The liver produces

    a. chylomicrons, lipase, and LDL.

    b. bile, HDL, and monoglycerides.

    c. VLDL, LDL, and HDL.

    d. diglycerides, chylomicrons, and lipoproteins.

2. The lipoprotein that helps to remove cholesterol from cells is

    a. chylomicrons.

    b. VLDL.

    c. LDL.

    d. HDL.

How Does Your Body Use Fat and Cholesterol?

✔ Know It

Check all of the statements that are true about how the body uses fat.

_____ source of energy

_____ cushions organs

_____ carries vitamin C and the B vitamins

_____ contributes to hardening of the arteries

_____ aids digestion

_____ part of cell membranes

_____ carries vitamins A, D, E, and K

✔ Find It

Put each of these terms or phrases under the correct category (some terms may be used more than once).

essential fatty acid   made by the liver   cell membranes   omega-3 fatty acid

blood clotting   eicosanoids   fish   vegetable oils   sex hormones

cell membranes

Linoleic Acid	Alpha-Linolenic Acid	Cholesterol

✔ Think About It

1. Your grandfather is taking fish oil supplements because he had heard that it was good for his heart. What can you tell him about this product?

    _____

    _____

2. What can he do to be heart healthy?

    _____

    _____

✔ Apply It

Take a trip to the pharmacy aisle at the grocery store. Find a supplement that is advertised as high in omega-3 fatty acids, EPA, and/or DHA. Complete the chart below. In addition, find the cost of each product in the chart.

Product	Omega-3 as EPA and/or DHA g	Cost
Tuna, light, 3 oz	0.2	
Salmon, 3 oz	2.3	

1. How does the supplement compare with tuna and salmon in grams of EPA and/or DHA?

2. Is the supplement worth the cost? Why or why not?

✔ Test It

1. Fat is the preferred fuel source of
   a. the heart, liver, and resting muscles.
   b. the brain, nervous system, and red blood cells.
   c. mucous membranes, skin, and hair.
   d. nothing—carbohydrate is the preferred fuel of all body systems and organs.

2. Linoleic acid is present in a high amount in
   a. fish.
   b. organ meats.
   c. vegetable oils and nuts.
   d. dairy products.

How Much (and What Types of) Fat Should You Eat?

✓ Know It

Put a plus (+) sign in front of fats you should include in your diet. Put a minus (–) sign in front of those you should limit.

_____ linoleic acid

_____ alpha-linolenic acid

_____ cholesterol

_____ monounsaturated fats

_____ saturated fats

_____ *trans* fats

✓ Find It

Fill in the blanks using these percentages and terms:

> 40 percent   33 percent   34 percent   fat   refined carbohydrates   calories

1. In the 1930s, Americans consumed _____ of their calories as fat.

2. In the 1960s, Americans consumed _____ of their calories as fat.

3. Currently, average Americans consume _____ of their calories as fat.

4. These numbers are misleading because _____ has increased 4 percent since the 1990s

   and _____ have increased 10 percent.

5. So Americans are eating more of both _____ and _____.

6. The primary source of calories is _____.

✔ Think About It

You signed up for a five-day-long winter camping trip. A sample menu is shown below.

Breakfast	**Lunch**	**Dinner**	**Pocket Snacks**
Oatmeal with raisins, brown sugar, and butter	Peanut butter or cheese on hard tack (rye crackers)	Dehydrated casserole with sausage added	Granola
Hot chocolate	Fruit leather	Hard tack	Chocolate pieces or cheese cubes

1. What is your impression of this menu? _____

    _____

2. Why would a menu be designed in this manner? _____

    _____

3. What would you add to this general menu that you would be willing to carry in your own backpack?

    _____

✔ Apply It

Interview an older relative or acquaintance. Find out what typical foods he or she ate at your age. Include questions about cooking methods and food processing. Compare this information to your own food choices today. What are at least three differences you can identify?

1. _____

2. _____

3. _____

✔ Test It

1. A low-fat diet would be considered _____ of daily calories from fat.

    a. 0 to 5 percent

    b. <20 percent

    c. 20 to 35 percent

    d. <50 percent

2. Dietary fat

    a. is not essential for health.

    b. is essential for health.

    c. increases body weight.

    d. contributes the same calories per gram as protein.

What Are the Best Food Sources of Fats?

✔ Know It

*Unsaturated or saturated? Indicate with a **U** if the food product contains primarily unsaturated fats. Use an **S** if the food product contains primarily saturated fats.*

_____ vegetable oils

_____ meat

_____ whole dairy products

_____ tree nuts (walnuts)

_____ flaxseed and wheat germ

_____ coconut and palm oil

_____ commercially made baked goods

✔ Find It

Check all of the food items that contain cholesterol.

_____	eggs	_____	cheese
_____	milk	_____	tofu
_____	avocado	_____	ice cream
_____	peanut butter	_____	gelatin
_____	shrimp	_____	turkey

✔ Think About It

You decided to try out a computerized diet analysis program. After entering data for what you ate over the weekend, the program computed 2,800 calories, 280 grams carbohydrate, 124 grams fat, and 140 grams protein.

1. How many fat calories does this equate to? _____

2. What percent of your total calories came from fat? _____

3. What changes do you think need to be made? _____

✔ Apply It

For each food item listed, suggest options with lower amounts of saturated fat.

Food Item	Lower Fat Option	Another Option
doughnut		
steak and cheese sub		
DQ Blizzard		
cheesy hash browns		
potato chips		
microwave popcorn with butter		

✔ Test It

1. You should _____ saturated fat in your diet.

    a. increase

    b. eliminate

    c. decrease

    d. moderate use of

2. Of the following foods, the one with the highest amount of cholesterol is

    a. an egg.

    b. organ meats.

    c. a hot dog.

    d. shrimp.

What Is *Trans* Fat and Where Do You Find It?

✔ Know It

Match each term to the appropriate definition.

_____	1. oxidation of fat causes decomposition	a.	*cis*
_____	2. chemically adding hydrogen to an unsaturated fat	b.	*trans*
_____	3. same	c.	rancidity
_____	4. cross	d.	hydrogenation

✔ Find It

Check all of the reasons why trans *fat has been used in the manufacturing of foods.*

_____   lower calories

_____   resistance to rancidity

_____   better texture

_____   decrease costs

_____   better for heart health

_____   replace saturated fat

✔ Find More

Check all of the products below that contain trans *fat.*

_____ breakfast cereals	_____ whole oats
_____ commercially baked goods	_____ vegetable salad
_____ hydrogenated shortening	_____ salad dressing
_____ fast-food fryers	_____ animal products
_____ fruit roll-ups	_____ potato chips

Looking at the list above, circle the group that contributes to most of the trans *fat in the average American diet. Put a rectangle around the food group that comes in second as a contributor of* trans *fat.*

✔ Think About It

After coming out of the nutrition lecture on types of fats and *trans* fats, you head to the cafeteria. You view the a la carte lunch menu. Thinking that you really should avoid foods with *trans* fat, you select (circle your lunch):

Cheeseburger on a Bun   Carrot Sticks   Milk Shake

Turkey/Cheese Wrap   Applesauce   Fountain Drink

Vegetable Pizza   Cream of Chicken Soup   Mineral Water

French Fries   Minestrone Soup

Why did you make those selections?

_____

_____

✔ Apply It

Analyze the nutrition information from a fast-food restaurant.

Menu Item	Calories	Total Fat	Saturated Fat	*Trans* Fat

1. Which item had the most fat? Saturated fat? *Trans* fat? _____

2. What information surprised you? _____

✓ Test It

1. The FDA _____ that *trans* fat _____.
    a. recommends; should be eliminated from the diet
    b. requires; be listed on the food label
    c. ignores; is in animal products
    d. suggests; be used in restaurant deep fat fryers

2. Hydrogenation
    a. makes food become rancid.
    b. increases the amount of polyunsaturated fats.
    c. decreases calories absorbed from fat.
    d. changes polyunsaturated fats into saturated fats.

What Are Fat Substitutes and How Can They Be Part of a Healthy Diet?

✓ Know It

Match each trade name product to the source and use.

_____	1. fat based; snack foods/chips	a.	Litesse
_____	2. carbohydrate based; thickening for baked goods	b.	Olean
_____	3. carbohydrate based; add bulk to baked goods	c.	Betatrim
_____	4. protein based; dairy products and frozen desserts	d.	Salatrim
_____	5. fat based; baked goods	e.	Simplesse

✔ Find It

Manufacturers have the ability to use chemically derived fat substitutes. These fat substitutes are not available for consumers to use in home cooking. There are, however, natural food products that may replace fat in some home recipes.

Unscramble the food names below to find out where each of the following alternatives to a fat could be used.

1. applesauce   snffumi   _____

2. low-fat milk   ashke   _____

3. vegetable spray attospeo   _____

4. pureed fruit   ekcosoi   _____

5. oatmeal   keca   _____

✔ Think About It

1. Circle the food item that you would choose in each of the following groupings.

    a. Lay's Original Potato Chips *or* Olean Chips *or* Baked Lays Potato Chips

    b. Sherbet *or* Simple Pleasures (Simplesse) *or* Ben & Jerry's Chocolate Chunk

    c. Fun Fruits *or* Fig Newtons *or* Fat-Free Fig Newtons

    d. Hamburger *or* Lean Hamburger *or* Diet Lean Hamburger

    e. Tomato/Lettuce *or* Reduced-Fat Cheese *or* Cheddar Cheese

2. Why did you make the choices that you did?

    _____

3. Did you always choose the lowest fat item? Why or why not?

    _____

    _____

✔ Apply It

Select two similar items at the grocery store—preferably a low-fat or fat-free item and then a comparable item (the textbook used the example of Fig Newtons and Fat-Free Fig Newtons). Fill in the Nutrition Facts for each product. Identify each item below its label.

Nutrition Facts

Serving Size
Servings Per Container

Amount Per Serving

Calories   Calories from Fat

% Daily Value*

Total Fat

   Saturated Fat

   Trans Fat

Cholesterol

Sodium

Total Carbohydrate

   Dietary Fiber

   Sugars

Protein

Vitamin A   •   Vitamin C

Calcium   • Iron   • Vitamin D

* Percent Daily Values are based on a 2,000 calorie diet. Your daily values may be higher or lower depending on your calorie needs:

Nutrition Facts

Serving Size
Servings Per Container

Amount Per Serving

Calories   Calories from Fat

% Daily Value*

Total Fat

   Saturated Fat

   Trans Fat

Cholesterol

Sodium

Total Carbohydrate

   Dietary Fiber

   Sugars

Protein

Vitamin A   •   Vitamin C

Calcium   • Iron   • Vitamin D

* Percent Daily Values are based on a 2,000 calorie diet. Your daily values may be higher or lower depending on your calorie needs:

Product:

Product:

_____   _____

1. How did the products compare? _____

2. Which one had more fat? _____

3. Which one had more carbohydrate? _____

4. Which one had more calories? _____

5. Which one would you want to buy to eat? _____

✔ Test It

1. Food products with fat substitutes

   a. can be consumed in twice the quantity of a comparable regular product.

   b. always save calories.

   c. can be enjoyed in moderation.

   d. are approved for use by the Department of Health.

2. Products containing Olestra

   a. have fat-soluble vitamins added.

   b. interfere with water-soluble nutrient absorption.

   c. include diet beverages.

   d. contain added calories from carbohydrate.

What Is Heart Disease and What Increases Your Risk?

✔ Know It

Match each term to the appropriate description.

_____	1. lack of oxygen resulting in damage to the heart muscle	a.	Syndrome X
_____	2. lack of oxygen to the brain	b.	heart attack
_____	3. narrowing of arteries	c.	hypertension
_____	4. buildup of foam cells, platelets, and waste products	d.	atherosclerosis
_____	5. high blood pressure	e.	risk factors
_____	6. likelihood of developing a disease	f.	plaque
_____	7. metabolic syndrome	g.	stroke

✔ Find It

*In the following list of risk factors for heart disease, mark **C** for risk factors that you can control and **X** for risk factors that you cannot control.*

_____   excess body weight

_____   age

_____   insulin sensitivity

_____   smoking

_____   physical inactivity

_____   type 1 diabetes

_____   low HDL cholesterol

_____   high LDL cholesterol

_____   family history of heart disease

_____   gender

_____   hypertension

Look at the list of risk factors above. Circle the risk factors that have a nutrition-related component.

✔ Think About It

You run into your favorite uncle at the corner pizza place. He tells you that he likes to get the large supreme pizza because then he has enough for lunch the next day. As he drives away, you observe him in his car smoking a pipe. You have always liked this uncle because he can ably play Santa Claus.

1. What risk factors can you identify in this uncle? _____

    _____

2. What lifestyle changes would you suggest that this uncle consider adopting? _____

    _____

✔ Apply It

Fill out this risk factor chart as completely as you can.

Risk Factor	You	Your Dad	His Dad (Your Paternal Grandfather)
insulin sensitivity			
hypertension			
tobacco use			
inactivity			
overweight			
high cholesterol			
heart disease			

1. Do you currently have any risk factors for heart disease? _____

2. How do you compare to your father and grandfather? _____

_____

3. Can you identify a family history of heart disease? _____

_____

4. What lifestyle changes do you plan to implement? _____

_____

✓ Test It

1. To lower LDL cholesterol
   a. drink wine with meals.
   b. increase physical activity.
   c. limit monounsaturated fats.
   d. limit homocysteine.

2. Syndrome X includes
   a. low LDL, high HDL cholesterol.
   b. hypoglycemia.
   c. abdominal obesity.
   d. decreased risk of heart disease.

What Is High Blood Cholesterol and What Can You Do to Lower It?

✓ Know It

Check each of the following factors that can help lower LDL cholesterol.

_____ increase saturated fat

_____ increase unsaturated fat

_____ limit *trans* fat

_____ include eggs daily

_____ include fruits and vegetables daily

_____ eat fish

_____ use fish oil supplements

_____ include nuts

✔ Find It

Circle all of the foods that contain cholesterol.

peanut butter   egg yolk   egg white   hamburger   broccoli   avocado

low-fat milk   orange   corn oil   chicken   soybeans   tofu   whole-

grain cereal   milk shake   chicken noodle soup

✔ Think About It

Your friend is bulking up for a bodybuilding competition. He is following a diet prepared by a trainer at the gym where he works out. During this phase of training the menu calls for six whole eggs plus six egg whites, 8 to 10 ounces of boiled chicken, fish oil supplements, no fruit, and limited vegetable intake. What nutrition concerns do you have for your friend?

_____

_____

_____

✔ Apply It

How often do you include foods in your diet that can help to lower cholesterol? Complete this food frequency questionnaire.

Food	Daily	At Least 2–3 Times per Week	At Least Monthly
vegetables			
fruits			
whole grains			
nuts			
fish			

What changes do you need to make to help your cholesterol remain in a healthy range?

_____

✔ Test It

1. Pregnant women are advised to avoid
   a. shrimp.
   b. canned light tuna.
   c. scallops.
   d. golden snapper or mackerel.

2. Alpha-linolenic acid is not found in
   a. flaxseeds.
   b. egg white.
   c. soybean and canola oil.
   d. walnuts.

Two Points of View

Farmed Salmon vs Wild Salmon: Is One Healthier Than the Other?

Read two professionals' opinions on this topic at the end of the chapter in your textbook, then consider the following questions:

1. According to the two experts, what contaminants can be found in fish?

   _____

   _____

2. Where do these contaminants come from?

   _____

   _____

3. What are the noted differences between farmed and wild salmon?

   _____

   _____

4. David Carpenter states that the "benefits of fish have been oversold." Why does he make this statement?

_____

_____

5. Do you agree with this statement? Why or why not?

_____

_____

6. What are Alex Trent's recommendations for fish consumption?

_____

_____

7. Which expert's view do you support? Why?

_____

_____

8. Does this discussion change your mind about including fish in your menu?

_____

_____

6

Proteins and Amino Acids

What Are Proteins?

✔ Know It

Complete the crossword puzzle using protein terms.

Across

1 bonds that connect amino acids
7 nutrients the body can synthesize
8 COOH group

Down

1 substance that precedes a step or reaction
2 nutrients that must come from the diet
3 carbon + hydrogen + oxygen + nitrogen
4 alteration of a protein's shape
5 nitrogen containing
6 nitrogen-containing waste product

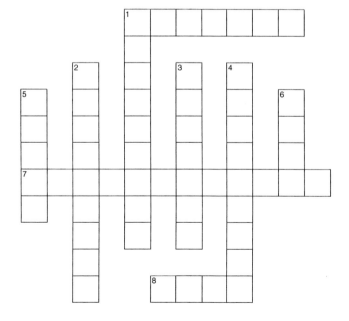

✔ Find It

Check all of the following foods that contain all nine essential amino acids.

_____   soybeans

_____   egg

_____   peanut butter

_____   milk

_____   pork chop

_____   mixed fruit

_____   butter

_____   bagel

✔ Think About It

The food court at the mall has a vendor that makes nutritional shakes. For an additional fee, you can have the following amino acids added: alanine, arginine, glutamine, or tyrosine.

1. Which of these amino acids would you choose to have added to a shake?

    _____

2. Why?

    _____

    _____

✔ Apply It

Proteins can be denatured by heat, acids, bases, or salts. List the protein foods you have eaten, or plan to eat, today. Which ones have been denatured prior to you consuming them? Complete the chart below.

Protein Food	Denatured? (Yes or No)	Method of Denaturation

✔ Test It

1. Unlike carbohydrates and fats, amino acids contain

    a. carbon.

    b. hydrogen.

    c. nitrogen.

    d. oxygen.

2. The differences between individual amino acids are attributed to the

    a. acid group.

    b. side chain.

    c. amine group.

    d. food source.

What Happens to the Protein You Eat?

✓ Know It

Match each term to the appropriate description.

_____ 1. stored supply of amino acids   a. DNA

_____ 2. process of breaking down and synthesizing protein   b. urea

_____ 3. nitrogen-containing waste product   c. gene

_____ 4. genetic blueprint in cells   d. RNA

_____ 5. DNA segment that codes for a specific protein   e. amino acid pool

_____ 6. carries out the orders of DNA   f. sickle-cell anemia

_____ 7. genetic defect in the development of hemoglobin   g. protein turnover

_____ 8. synthesis of amino acids is equal to excretion   h. protein balance

✓ Find It

Number, in order from 1 to 5, the process of protein digestion.

_____ Amino acids are absorbed into the blood.

_____ Acidic juices denature protein.

_____ Nitrogen is excreted in the urine.

_____ Polypeptides are broken down into tripeptides and dipeptides.

_____ Amino acids are used to make new proteins or glucose.

✔ Think About It

A couple of your friends have joined a bodybuilding class. One of them heard that bodybuilders need to ingest a lot of extra protein in order to "bulk up." According to him, the only way to know if you are getting enough is when there is extra nitrogen in the urine. To test for this, he purchased some urine testing sticks. According to his claims, they must turn bright green before you are assured of taking in an adequate amount of protein. What do you think of this technique?

_____

_____

_____

✔ Apply It

Look at the labels of various food, cosmetic, and pharmaceutical products. Identify added amino acids.

Name of Product	Amino Acids Added

Which of these findings surprised you? Why?

_____

_____

_____

✔ Test It

1. Protein digestion begins in the
   a. mouth.
   b. stomach.
   c. small intestine.
   d. gallbladder.

2. The enzyme, pepsin, is activated in the
   a. mouth.
   b. stomach.
   c. liver.
   d. pancreas.

How Does Your Body Use Proteins?

✔ Know It

Match the terms to the appropriate role of protein.

_____	1. collagen; connective tissue	a.	transport
_____	2. speed up reactions in the body	b.	fluid balance
_____	3. even dispersion of water	c.	antibodies; immunity
_____	4. concentration of hydrogen ions	d.	energy
_____	5. carry oxygen, waste products, and nutrients	e.	structural support
_____	6. attack pathogens	f.	acid-base balance; buffer
_____	7. provide calories	g.	enzymes; hormones

✔ Find It

Circle the words in the puzzle that relate to how the body uses protein.

ANTIBODIES   EDEMA   IMMUNITY
BALANCE   ENERGY   MAINTENANCE
BUFFER   ENZYME   STRUCTURE
CATALYST   HORMONE   TRANSPORT

```
S  K  Y  A  Z  A  X  H  J  T  B  E  C  L  C
M  E  X  G  M  T  O  C  E  R  A  M  V  W  E
C  G  I  E  R  R  K  R  N  O  L  Y  G  Y  Q
E  A  D  D  M  E  U  M  X  P  A  Z  D  O  A
N  E  T  O  O  T  N  T  R  S  N  N  D  G  U
C  H  N  A  C  B  P  E  P  N  C  E  M  Z  C
G  E  D  U  L  Q  I  V  O  A  E  Z  N  R  N
Z  M  R  L  N  Y  F  T  H  R  E  F  F  U  B
V  T  J  X  Q  R  S  F  N  T  G  I  T  U  O
S  Q  I  X  W  W  L  T  J  A  L  K  C  U  Z
I  M  M  U  N  I  T  Y  R  B  A  N  R  I  N
E  O  P  H  P  N  H  R  C  Y  H  X  V  V  U
J  C  J  F  K  I  V  R  N  S  W  O  L  P  P
G  R  Y  O  K  I  Z  M  Y  E  D  G  A  T  H
R  P  Y  E  C  N  A  N  E  T  N  I  A  M  E
```

✔ Think About It

1. A classmate, who is recovering from anorexia, says that as soon as she eats a meal, her feet and lower legs swell. What role of protein could this be attributed to?

   _____

2. Another classmate said that his physician did not want to give him a measles vaccine because he was just getting over a viral infection. What role of protein would the physician be concerned with?

   _____

✔ Apply It

List all of the between-meal foods, snacks, and beverages you ate today. Look at the food labels for protein and calories. Calculate the protein calories and the percent of calories from protein to complete the chart below.

Food Item	Protein, g	Protein Calories	Total Calories	Percent of Calories from Protein

How would you summarize your protein intake from snacks?

_____

_____

✓ Test It

1. _____ is the term used when the space between cells becomes bloated and body tissue swells.

   a. Enzyme

   b. Hormone

   c. Antibody

   d. Edema

2. Proteins act as _____ to help keep the pH of your body fluids balanced.

   a. enzymes

   b. buffers

   c. hormones

   d. transports

How Much Protein Do You Need and What Are Protein-Rich Food Sources?

✓ Know It

Match each term with the appropriate definition.

_____	1. food's capacity to be broken down and absorbed	a.	amino acid profile
_____	2. measure of digestibility and meeting of body needs	b.	complete
_____	3. composition of amino acids	c.	limiting
_____	4. provides all the essential amino acids	d.	digestibility
_____	5. protein from plant sources	e.	incomplete
_____	6. amino acid in shortest supply	f.	complemented
_____	7. combining sources of incomplete proteins	g.	protein quality

✔ Find It

Use **C** if the food in the list below contains complete proteins (all of the essential amino acids). Use **I** if the food contains primarily incomplete proteins.

_____	low-fat milk	_____	pear
_____	green beans	_____	Colby cheese
_____	hummus	_____	peanut butter
_____	whole-grain bread	_____	baked potato
_____	pork chop	_____	rye crackers
_____	salmon	_____	rice

✔ Think About It

Using the list of foods above, put together four combinations of incomplete proteins that together would complement each other to make a complete protein.

1. _____ + _____

2. _____ + _____

3. _____ + _____

4. _____ + _____

✔ Apply It

Calculate your daily protein need.

1. Convert your body weight from pounds to kilograms.

   your weight in pounds: _____ lb ÷ 2.2 = _____ kg

2. Multiply your weight in kilograms by 0.8 grams.

   your weight in kilograms: _____ × 0.8 g = _____ g/day

✔ Test It

1. Protein quality is determined by

   a. complete and complementary proteins.

   b. the amino acid profile.

   c. positive nitrogen balance.

   d. digestibility and essential and/or nonessential amino acids.

2. Negative nitrogen balance commonly occurs in

   a. infants and pregnant women.

   b. anorexics.

   c. muscle-building athletes.

   d. growing teenagers.

What Happens if You Eat Too Much or Too Little Protein?

✔ Know It

First, fill in the letter blanks to spell out each term that is described. Then fill in the letter blanks for the phrase below using the associated numbered letters.

__ __ __ __ __ __ __   __ __ F __ __ __ __ __ __ __
 6 3 5 2 7 4 1   10 7   4 9 4 7 1 9 8

M A L __ U __ __ __ __ __ __ __   inadequate nutrition
         1   2 3 4 2 4 5 1

K W A S H __ __ __ K __ __   PEM with severe protein deficiency
               4 5 3   5 3

M A __ A S M U S   starvation
       3

__ __ M   lack of sufficient protein and/or calories
 6 7

__ __ __ __ G __   calories
 7 1 7 3   8

__ H __ L __ __ __ __   most at risk for PEM
 9   4   10 3 7 1

✔ Find It

Look at the symptoms and disease states listed below. Use a plus (+) sign if the condition is due to eating too much protein. Use a minus (−) sign if the condition is related to eating too little protein. (It is possible to use both signs for a single condition.)

_____ increased risk of heart disease

_____ compromised immune status

_____ loss of cells in the GI tract

_____ osteoporosis

_____ emaciated appearance

_____ kidney stones

_____ obesity

_____ edema

✔ Think About It

You were assigned to work with a group of students that you did not know. One member of the group appeared shy and sad. She always sat in the back of the classroom and did not actively participate during lectures. Her sweat suits hung off of her frail-looking body. When your group met over lunch, she brought half of a cucumber.

1. Do you think your group member is suffering from a protein deficiency?

    _____

    _____

2. If so, which deficiency would you think your group member is exhibiting?

    _____

    _____

✔ Apply It

Estimate your protein intake. Write down everything you ate yesterday. Tally up the number of servings that you had from each food group and fill in the chart below.

_____ milk servings × 8 g per serving =   _____ g

_____ vegetable servings × 2 g per serving =   _____ g

_____ grains, cereal servings × 2 g per serving = _____ g

_____ protein alternative × 7 g per serving =   _____ g

_____ meat, fish, poultry × 7 g per ounce =   _____ g

_____ fruit servings × 0 g per serving =   0   g

_____ other   _____ g

                                                   _____ TOTAL g

1. What was the estimated amount of protein that you ate yesterday?

    _____

    _____

2. How does that compare to your protein recommendation (you calculated this in the previous section)?

    _____

    _____

3. What changes do you need to make with regard to your protein intake?

    _____

    _____

✔ Test It

1. Eating a high-protein diet can
    a. help weight-loss efforts.
    b. increase HDL and decrease LDL cholesterol.
    c. increase total cholesterol.
    d. cause diarrhea.

2. A severe deficiency of protein is termed
    a. kwashiorkor.
    b. marasmus.
    c. PEM.
    d. starvation.

How Do Vegetarians Meet Their Protein Needs?

✔ Know It

Match each type of vegetarianism to the typical meal plans.

_____ 1. includes dairy foods, nuts, legumes   a. ovo-vegetarian

_____ 2. includes dairy foods, eggs, legumes   b. vegan

_____ 3. includes eggs, nuts, legumes, vegetables   c. semivegetarian

_____ 4. avoids use of any animal product   d. lacto-vegetarian

_____ 5. occasionally includes meat, fish, poultry   e. lacto-ovo-vegetarian

✔ Find It

Arrange the following food items under the various vegetarian meal plans. Food items may be used in more than one column.

goat's-milk cheese   orange   tuna fish   tempeh   yogurt   broccoli

sunflower seeds   soy milk   omelet   fruit juice   whole-grain bread

ice cream   sorbet

Lacto-Vegetarian	Lacto-Ovo-Vegetarian	Semivegetarian	Vegan

✔ Think About It

The dormitory food committee is meeting with the food service director. The main agenda item is that students want vegetarian options available at every meal. The food service director contends that this request is being met with a salad bar and make-your-own sandwiches. The salad bar always includes low-fat cottage cheese, peas or garbanzo beans, and an assortment of greens. The sandwich fixings always include peanut butter and cheese.

1. Do you think this is adequate nutrition for dormitory students following vegetarian meal plans?

   _____

2. What will you suggest to the food service director at the next meeting?

   _____

✔ Apply It

Select a menu from a restaurant where you frequently eat.

1. If you were following a lacto-ovo-vegetarian plan, what could you select for a meal?

   _____

   _____

2. If you were following a vegan plan, what could you select from the menu?

   _____

   _____

3. Would you consider these meals adequate calorically and nutritionally? Why or why not?

   _____

   _____

✔ Test It

1. Vegetarians
   a. tend to have heart disease at the same rate as nonvegetarians.
   b. have increased risk of various types of cancer.
   c. have lower blood pressure.
   d. tend to exhibit disordered eating behaviors.

2. A vegan could assure adequate calcium in his or her diet by
   a. adding milk to cereal.
   b. eating green vegetables.
   c. snacking on cheese.
   d. adding beans to salads.

Two Points of View

Do You Need to Eat Meat to Compete?

Read two professionals' opinions on this topic at the end of the chapter in your textbook, then consider the following questions:

1. According to the two experts, which should come first, adequate protein or calories? Why?

2. What nutrient deficiencies can occur in vegetarians?

3. Who is most at risk in following a vegetarian diet: a gymnast or a bodybuilder? Why?

4. How can inadequate iron affect physical performance?

5. What foods provide vitamin B_{12}?

6. What are the possible consequences of vitamin B_{12} deficiency?

7. What do you note about the credentials of the experts?

Vitamins

What Are Vitamins?

✔ Know It

Check all of the facts that are true of vitamins.

_____ organic

_____ inorganic

_____ essential

_____ nonessential

_____ amount needed is small

_____ stored in the body

_____ excreted easily from the body

_____ calorie containing

_____ fat soluble

_____ water soluble

✔ Know It, Too

*Use a **W** to identify vitamins that are water soluble. Use an **F** to identify vitamins that are fat soluble.*

vitamin A

vitamin B_6

vitamin D

vitamin K

vitamin E

vitamin C

biotin

niacin

thiamin, riboflavin

vitamin B_{12}

folate

✔ Find It

Select the best handling practices to preserve vitamins in foods.

_____   keep produce at room temperature

_____   freeze produce

_____   boil vegetables

_____   refrigerate vegetables

_____   store in airtight containers

_____   can fruits

_____   microwave vegetables

_____   shop for produce frequently and use quickly

_____   steam vegetables

✔ Think About It

If you live in a northern climate where it is not possible to grow produce in the winter, what products would you use to get the most vitamin nutrition: canned, frozen, fresh shipped from another country, or root vegetables grown last summer? Why?

_____

_____

_____

_____

✔ Apply It

Go through your cupboard and refrigerator. List food items and their form (fresh, frozen, canned, and so on). Note how long you have had that item and when you plan to use it.

Food Item	Fresh, Frozen, Canned, or Dehydrated	Length of Time Since Purchase	Length of Time Between Purchase and Use

1. Are you getting all of the vitamins out of the foods you purchase?

   _____

2. What have you learned?

   _____

   _____

3. Which products should you use quickly or discard?

   _____

   _____

   _____

✔ Test It

1. Vitamins
   a. contain amines.
   b. are inorganic.
   c. are organic.
   d. provide energy.

2. Fat-soluble vitamins are
   a. absorbed in the lymph.
   b. absorbed directly into the bloodstream.
   c. not stored in excess in the body.
   d. nonessential.

Vitamin A

✔ Know It

Match each term to the appropriate description.

_____	1. can be converted to retinal and retinoic acid	a.	provitamin A
_____	2. found only in animal sources	b.	hypervitaminosis A
_____	3. found in plant sources	c.	carotenodermia
_____	4. measure of vitamin A	d.	retinol
_____	5. toxic level of vitamin A in liver	e.	xerophthalmia
_____	6. result of eating too many carotenoids	f.	retinol activity equivalents
_____	7. deficiency leading to cornea damage	g.	night blindness

✔ Find It

Check each of the following that provides a source of vitamin A.

_____ potato   _____ cheese

_____ squash   _____ eggs

_____ apple   _____ green leafy vegetables

_____ yam, sweet potato   _____ celery

_____ milk   _____ carrots

✔ Think About It

One of your roommates is dieting to lose weight. She is starting to look a peculiar shade of orange. Your other roommates think she is secretly drinking a lot of alcohol and developing a liver disorder. What would you suspect is the real problem?

_____

_____

✔ Apply It

1. List all of the foods you have eaten today.

_____

_____

_____

2. Circle all of the foods in your list above that contain a source of vitamin A. What changes should you make in your vitamin A intake?

_____

✔ Test It

1. Preformed vitamin A is found in

   a. carrots.

   b. spinach.

   c. eggs.

   d. fruit juice.

2. Vitamin A deficiency is the number-one cause of _____ in _____.

   a. heart disease; women

   b. blindness; children

   c. skin cancer; young adults

   d. anemia; elderly people

Vitamin E

✔ Know It

Fill in the blanks using these terms.

anticoagulant   antioxidant   hemorrhage   alpha-tocopherol

1. The most active form of natural vitamin E is _____.

2. Vitamin E is a(n) _____ because it inhibits blood clotting.

3. Vitamin E is a(n) _____ that has a role in protecting cell membranes.

4. Excess vitamin E in the body increases the risk of _____, or excessive bleeding.

✔ Find It

Check each of the following that provides a source of vitamin E.

_____   vegetable oil   _____   orange

_____   water   _____   soy milk

_____   wheat germ   _____   avocado

_____   nuts and seeds   _____   tomato

✔ Think About It

You received an advertisement for vitamin E supplements in the mail. The ad states that you need extra vitamin E for its antioxidant properties, particularly if you live in smoggy or smoke-filled environments, don't eat vegetables, or are on a low-fat diet.

What do you think of the claims in this advertisement?

_____

_____

✔ Apply It

Add food items to each of the following to increase vitamin E.

1. iceberg head lettuce + _____

2. whole-grain crackers + _____

3. raisins and chocolate chips + _____

4. oatmeal + _____

✔ Test It

1. Fat malabsorption can result in a deficiency of
    a. vitamin E.
    b. vitamin C.
    c. thiamin and riboflavin.
    d. folate.

2. An anticoagulant
    a. protects cell membranes.
    b. can cause hemorrhage.
    c. inhibits platelets from clumping together.
    d. leads to increased vitamin absorption.

Vitamin K

✔ Know It

Circle the correct answer of the choices given in each of the following statements.

1. Menaquinone is (synthesized by intestinal bacteria *or* found in green plants).

2. Phylloquinone is (synthesized by intestinal bacteria *or* found in green plants).

3. Acting as a (coenzyme *or* hormone), vitamin K alters bone protein.

4. (Inadequate *or* Excess) dietary vitamin K may be a factor in osteoporosis.

5. There are (many *or* no) known effects of consuming too much vitamin K.

6. Warfarin (increases *or* decreases) the activity of vitamin K.

✔ Find It

Check the following that provide a source of vitamin K.

kiwi   asparagus   intestinal bacteria

spinach   apple juice   sunlight

milk   chicken   water

olive oil   cabbage   margarine

✔ Think About It

At birth, infants are commonly given a dose of vitamin K. Why do you think this has become a common medical practice?

_____

_____

✔ Apply It

Add foods to each of the following to increase vitamin K.

1. crusty french bread + _____

2. iceberg lettuce + _____

3. carrots + _____

4. potato + _____

✔ Test It

1. Effects of consuming too much vitamin K include
    a. no known effects.
    b. atherosclerosis.
    c. osteoporosis.
    d. blood clots.

2. Vitamin K is essential for

    a. eyesight.

    b. coagulation.

    c. mucous membranes.

    d. healthy hair and nails.

Vitamin D

✔ Know It

Circle the correct answer of the choices given in each of the following statements.

1. A nonfood source of vitamin D is (intestinal bacteria *or* sunlight).

2. When vitamin D from food enters the body, it is in an (active *or* inactive) form.

3. When vitamin D from sunlight enters the body, it is in an (active *or* inactive) form.

4. Vitamin D acts as a (hormone *or* coenzyme) to regulate calcium in the blood.

5. Breast, colon, and prostate cancers are (more prominent *or* less frequent) in individuals living in sunny regions.

6. Vitamin D may help (prevent *or* increase) diabetes mellitus.

7. The vitamin D deficiency in children is called (rickets *or* osteomalacia).

8. Daily vitamin recommendations (include *or* do not include) synthesis of vitamin D from sunlight.

✔ Find It

Check any of the following that could be reasons for the increased incidence of rickets in children.

_____ drinking fortified milk   _____ increased consumption of soft drinks

_____ concern over skin cancer   _____ limited intake of fruit

_____ limited outdoor activities   _____ organized sports

_____ increased fat consumption   _____ air pollution

✔ Think About It

Check the cities where vitamin D production from sunlight might be limited during winter months.

Minneapolis, MN	San Diego, CA	Kansas City, MO
Dallas, TX	Des Moines, IA	Atlanta, GA
St. Louis, MO	Phoenix, AZ	Madison, WI
Detroit, MI	Boston, MA	Big Sky, MT
Seattle, WA	Grand Forks, ND	Denver, CO

✔ Apply It

Add foods to each of the following to increase vitamin D.

1. granola and fruit + _____

2. mixed salad greens + _____

3. fresh berries + _____

4. coffee + _____

✔ Test It

1. Hypercalcemia is
    a. caused by inadequate vitamin D.
    b. a high amount of calcium in the blood.
    c. the adult form of vitamin D deficiency.
    d. caused by chronic sunburns.

2. Vitamin D is generally found in
    a. green leafy vegetables.
    b. lean meat products.
    c. fresh fruits.
    d. dairy products.

Thiamin (B₁)

✔ Know It

Check the correct answer(s) for each of the following statements.

1. Thiamin

   _____ was the first B vitamin discovered.

   _____ is sensitive to light.

   _____ is used in high doses as a drug to treat high cholesterol.

2. Thiamin is needed for

   _____ healthy skin cells.

   _____ nerve function.

   _____ energy metabolism.

   _____ functioning of the digestive system.

3. The deficiency of thiamin is

   _____ a condition affecting tissues of the throat, mouth, and tongue.

   _____ known as pellagra.

   _____ known as beriberi.

✔ Find It

Check all of the following that provide thiamin.

_____ apple   _____ enriched rice

_____ green beans   _____ turkey

_____ pork loin   _____ cheddar cheese

_____ whole-grain cereal   _____ soybeans

Circle the food item that provides the richest source of thiamin.

✔ Think About It

Is it possible for a college student to develop Wernicke-Korsakoff syndrome? Why or why not?

_____

_____

_____

✔ Apply It

Add foods to each of the following to increase thiamin.

1. yogurt + _____

2. vegetable beef soup with _____

3. mashed potatoes + _____

4. toast + _____

✔ Test It

1. Toxicity symptoms of too much thiamin
    a. include loss of appetite and weight loss.
    b. lead to polyneuritis.
    c. are not known.
    d. are seen in alcohol intoxication.

2. Thiamin is found in
    a. orange juice, doughnuts, and tea.
    b. pasta, peas, and pork.
    c. peanut butter, celery sticks, and raisins.
    d. popcorn, pretzels, and beer.

Riboflavin (B₂)

✓ Know It

Check the correct answer(s) for each of the following statements.

1. Riboflavin

   _____ was the first B vitamin discovered.

   _____ is sensitive to light.

   _____ is used in high doses as a drug to treat high cholesterol.

2. Riboflavin is needed for

   _____ healthy skin cells.

   _____ nerve function.

   _____ energy metabolism.

   _____ functioning of the digestive system.

3. The deficiency of riboflavin

   _____ affects the tissues of the throat, mouth, and tongue.

   _____ is called pellagra.

   _____ is called beriberi.

✓ Find It

Check all of the following foods that are sources of riboflavin.

_____	pear	_____	enriched cereal
_____	fresh greens	_____	yogurt
_____	cheese pizza	_____	soybeans
_____	scrambled egg	_____	pork chop

✓ Think About It

List typical foods college students consume that provide adequate sources of riboflavin.

_____

_____

✓ Apply It

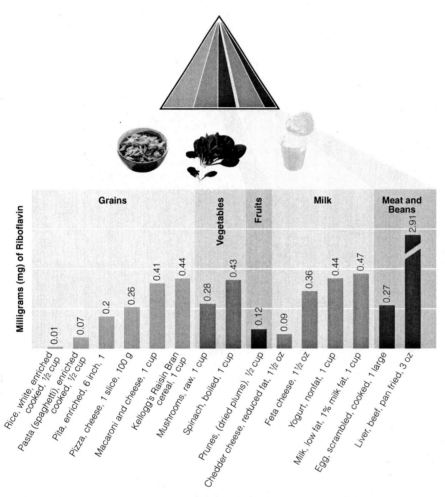

(Refer to page 229 in your textbook for a full-color version of this image.)

Complete the chart to meet your needs for riboflavin.

Food Item	Additional Food Item	Additional Food Item	Daily Need Males 1.3 mg Females 1.1 mg
2 slices pizza 0.52 mg			
1 cup yogurt 0.44 mg			
2 cups pasta 0.28 mg			

✔ Test It

1. Consuming too much riboflavin

    a. will turn urine yellow.

    b. is toxic.

    c. interferes with vitamin D.

    d. can cure a hangover.

2. To protect the riboflavin in milk, it should

    a. be stored in glass bottles.

    b. be stored in opaque containers.

    c. not be pasteurized.

    d. be fortified with vitamin A.

Niacin (B₃)

✔ Know It

Check the correct answer(s) for each of the following statements.

1. Niacin

   _____ was the first B vitamin discovered.

   _____ is sensitive to light.

   _____ is used in high doses as a drug to treat high cholesterol.

2. Niacin is needed for

   _____ healthy skin cells.

   _____ nerve function.

   _____ energy metabolism.

   _____ functioning of the digestive system.

3. The deficiency of niacin

   _____ affects the tissues of the throat, mouth, and tongue.

   _____ is called pellagra.

   _____ is called beriberi.

✔ Find It

Check all of the following that are sources of niacin.

_____ kiwi   _____ green beans

_____ Cheerios   _____ corn

_____ pasta   _____ enriched rice

_____ chicken   _____ tuna fish

✔ Think About It

Your friend has been preparing for a bodybuilding competition. One of the practices that he commonly follows is to take a high-dose niacin supplement prior to performing.

1. Why would he do this?

     _____

     _____

2. What do you think of this practice? Why?

     _____

     _____

     _____

3. Your skin has been dry all winter. Your physician has called it "dermatitis." Do you think this could be a beginning symptom of pellagra? Why or why not?

     _____

     _____

✔ Apply It

Add foods to each of the following to increase niacin.

1. whole-wheat bread + _____

2. M & Ms + _____

3. pasta + _____

4. salad greens + _____

✔ Test It

1. Niacin can be synthesized from the amino acid
   a. arginine.
   b. histidine.
   c. creatine.
   d. tryptophan.

2. Niacin has been shown to
   a. cause cancer.
   b. lower HDL cholesterol.
   c. lower LDL cholesterol.
   d. increase absorption of fat.

Vitamin B₆

✔ Know It

Match each term to the appropriate definition.

_____ 1. plant form of vitamin B₆   a. anemia

_____ 2. animal food source of vitamin B₆   b. pyridoxine

_____ 3. blood disorder   c. hemoglobin

_____ 4. blood protein   d. pyridoxal

✔ Find It

Check all of the following that provide vitamin B₆.

_____ broccoli   _____ chicken

_____ baked potato   _____ spinach

_____ banana   _____ flavored water

_____ hamburger   _____ kidney beans

✔ Think About It

Your friend says she suffers from premenstrual syndrome. Her mother told her to take supplements of vitamin B$_6$ two weeks before her period. What do you think of this recommendation?

_____

✔ Apply It

Add food items to each of the following to increase vitamin B$_6$.

1. milk + _____

2. whole-grain bread + _____

3. apples + _____

4. salad greens + _____

✔ Test It

1. Vitamin B$_6$ acts as a coenzyme
   a. in the metabolism of protein.
   b. in the making of hemoglobin.
   c. to treat carpal tunnel syndrome.
   d. to alleviate depression.

2. Nerve damage has been associated with
   a. vitamin B$_6$ deficiency.
   b. vitamin B$_6$ toxicity.
   c. anemia.
   d. both a and b.

Folate

✔ Know It

Match each term to the appropriate description.

_____	1. naturally occurring B vitamin in foods	a.	anencephaly
_____	2. synthetic form of folate	b.	folic acid
_____	3. spine, brain, skull	c.	spina bifida
_____	4. incompletely formed brain	d.	megaloblasts
_____	5. improperly developed backbone and spinal cord	e.	folate
_____	6. large immature cells	f.	macrocytes
_____	7. abnormally large red blood cells	g.	neural tube

✔ Find It

Check all of the following that provide folate.

_____	orange juice	_____	whole-grain bread
_____	green leafy vegetables	_____	pasta
_____	yogurt	_____	margarine
_____	potato	_____	cold cereal

✔ Think About It

1. Calculate the dietary folate equivalent (DFE) for a pizza crust mix in which the label states 80 micrograms of folic acid per serving.

   _____

2. What could be added to this product to increase folate?

   _____

✔ Apply It

Add food items to the following to increase folate.

1. milk + _____

2. lettuce + _____

3. chicken + _____

4. yogurt + _____

✔ Test It

1. Naturally occurring folate can be found in
    a. asparagus.
    b. pasta.
    c. breakfast cereal.
    d. oat bran muffins.

2. Folate is thought to
    a. increase the risk of lung cancer.
    b. lower the risk of colon cancer.
    c. cause birth defects.
    d. raise LDL cholesterol.

Vitamin B$_{12}$

✔ Know It

Circle the correct answer of the choices given in each of the following statements.

1. Vitamin B$_{12}$ is also called (folic acid *or* cobalamin).

2. Vitamin B$_{12}$ is a (water *or* fat)-soluble vitamin that (can *or* cannot) be stored in the liver.

3. Intrinsic factor is a(n) (enzyme *or* protein) needed to promote vitamin B$_{12}$ absorption.

4. The ability to absorb naturally occurring vitamin B$_{12}$ (increases *or* decreases) with age.

5. Vitamin B$_{12}$ is found primarily in (animal *or* plant) foods.

✔ Find It

Check all of the following that provide vitamin B$_{12}$.

_____ banana   _____ pork chop

_____ milk   _____ orange juice

_____ spinach   _____ shrimp

_____ tuna fish   _____ egg

✔ Think About It

1. You have an elderly relative who receives monthly injections of vitamin B$_{12}$. What condition does your relative have?

   _____

   _____

2. Could a better diet improve this situation? Why or why not?

   _____

   _____

   _____

✔ Apply It

Add food items to increase vitamin B$_{12}$.

1. broccoli + _____

2. pineapple + _____

3. bread + _____

4. boiled potatoes + _____

✔ Test It

1. Vegetarians can get vitamin B_{12} from
   a. intrinsic factor.
   b. injection.
   c. fortified soy products.
   d. nuts and legumes.

2. Pernicious anemia is most common in
   a. infants.
   b. weight-conscious adolescents.
   c. athletes.
   d. elderly people.

Vitamin C

✔ Know It

Circle the correct answer of the choices given in each of the following statements.

1. Vitamin C is also known as (folic acid *or* ascorbic acid).

2. Vitamin C acts as a (hormone *or* coenzyme) needed to synthesize some amino acids.

3. Vitamin C also acts as an (antioxidant *or* enzyme), which may help reduce the risk of chronic diseases.

4. Vitamin C is found primarily in (plant *or* animal) foods.

5. The vitamin C deficiency is called (anemia *or* scurvy).

✔ Find It

Check all of the following that provide vitamin C.

_____ tomato   _____ broccoli

_____ potato   _____ pasta

_____ hamburger   _____ cottage cheese

_____ bran flakes   _____ watermelon

✔ Think About It

Two of your friends are having a disagreement over taking vitamin C supplements. Erick is taking 50 milligrams in the form of a cough lozenge. Julia is taking a 3,200-milligram supplement she purchased at a health food store. Each believes their choice is the better one.

1. What do you think of your friends' supplement use?

    _____

    _____

2. What are possible side effects of Erick's supplement?

    _____

3. What are possible side effects of Julia's supplement?

    _____

✔ Apply It

Add food items to increase vitamin C.

1. apple and pear + _____

2. turkey sandwich with _____

3. frozen yogurt + _____

4. corn flakes + _____

✔ Test It

1. People who smoke

    a. absorb more vitamin C.

    b. commonly suffer from hemochromatosis.

    c. need additional vitamin C.

    d. should avoid vitamin C supplements.

2. Vitamin C

    a. can act as a hormone.

    b. reduces absorption of iron from grain foods.

    c. breaks down collagen.

    d. enables the body to make white blood cells.

Pantothenic Acid and Biotin

✔ Know It

Circle the correct answer of the choices given in the following statements.

1. Pantothenic acid and biotin are (water *or* fat)-soluble vitamins.

2. The primary functions of pantothenic acid and biotin are to aid in (energy *or* vitamin) metabolism.

3. Most Americans (easily meet *or* are deficient in) their pantothenic acid and biotin needs.

4. Biotin can be synthesized by (sunlight *or* intestinal bacteria).

5. Pantothenic acid and biotin are found in (meat *or* a wide variety of food products).

✔ Find It

Check all of the following that provide pantothenic acid or biotin.

_____   eggs

_____   peanut butter

_____   bran flakes

_____   milk

_____   mozzarella cheese

_____   turkey

_____   orange juice

_____   broccoli

✔ Think About It

You found a pamphlet at the gym with a recipe for making eggnog for weight lifters. The recipe calls for milk, eight to ten raw egg whites, and flavoring. What do you think of this recipe?

_____

_____

_____

✔ Test It

1. Pantothenic acid and biotin deficiencies

   a. are not common.

   b. occur frequently in infants.

   c. can be found in the elderly.

   d. occur frequently in vegetarians.

2. To ensure adequate intake of pantothenic acid and biotin,

   a. eat eggs three times per week.

   b. use supplements.

   c. eat enriched grain products.

   d. eat a healthy balanced diet.

Are There Other Important Nutrients?

✔ Know It

Match each term to the appropriate description.

_____ 1. essential for healthy cells and nerves   a. carnitine

_____ 2. needed to utilize fat   b. inositol

_____ 3. helps cells generate energy   c. choline

_____ 4. needed for healthy cell membranes   d. lipoic acid

Find It

List each food under the nutrients that it contains.

dairy products   meat   plant foods   eggs   peanuts

Choline	Carnitine	Inositol

✔ Think About It

You attended a symposium on running at which one of the speakers advocated the use of carnitine to help improve performance. A two-week supply was given to you free of charge.

1. Will you try it out? Why or why not?

2. Will you purchase the two-month supply recommended? Why or why not?

✔ Apply It

Visit a health food store and look for products that list choline, carnitine, inositol, and lipoic acid on their labels.

Product Name	Choline	Carnitine	Inositol	Lipoic Acid

1. What kinds of claims were on the labels of these products?

   _____

   _____

   _____

   _____

2. What did you learn?

   _____

   _____

   _____

   _____

✔ Test It

1. Low blood pressure is referred to as
   a. hypertension.
   b. hypotension.
   c. hyperthermia.
   d. hypothermia.

2. _____ is an essential nutrient needed for healthy cells and nerves.
   a. Choline
   b. Carnitine
   c. Lipoic acid
   d. Inositol

What Are Antioxidants?

✓ Know It

Match each term to the appropriate description.

_____ 1. counteract oxygen-containing free radicals

_____ 2. colorful pigments found in fruits and vegetables

_____ 3. process during which oxygen combines with other molecules

_____ 4. unstable oxygen-containing molecules

_____ 5. negatively charged particle in an atom

_____ 6. condition in which free radicals accumulate faster than the body can neutralize them

_____ 7. naturally occurring plant compounds

a. electron

b. oxidation

c. phytochemicals

d. antioxidants

e. oxidative stress

f. free radicals

g. flavonoids

✓ Find It

In the following three menus, circle the foods that provide phytochemicals.

Orange Juice	Ham and Cheese	Coleslaw
Bagel	on Whole Wheat	Soy Burger
Green Tea	Lettuce, Tomato, Onion	Broccoli
Butter	Apple	Rice Pilaf
	Milk	Red Wine

✓ Think About It

Your grandmother has a difficult time distinguishing you from your siblings and cousins due to age-related macular degeneration.

1. Do you need to worry about this condition? _____

2. What can you do to reduce the possibility of developing this condition?

_____

✔ Apply It

1. Write down your menu for tomorrow.

    _____

    _____

    _____

    _____

    _____

2. Circle the foods that contain phytochemicals. What else can you add to your menu to increase phyto-chemicals?

    _____

    _____

    _____

✔ Test It

1. For the health of your eyes, eat
    a. whole-grain cereal and low-fat milk.
    b. crackers, cheese, and wine.
    c. eggs, hash browns, and lean ham.
    d. oranges, broccoli, and spinach.

2. Flavonoids can be found in
    a. dairy products.
    b. fruits and vegetables.
    c. eggs.
    d. meat products.

How Should You Get Your Vitamins?

✓ Know It

Check each of the following if the nutrient listed is a fortified part of the food item.

_____   calcium in milk

_____   calcium in orange juice

_____   lycopene in tomato sauce

_____   vitamins A and D in milk

_____   vitamin C in fruit drink

_____   folic acid in cereal

_____   potassium in potato

_____   vitamin A in carrots

_____   riboflavin in milk

✓ Find It

Check all of the following people who may benefit from a nutrient supplement.

_____   a woman planning a pregnancy

_____   typical college student

_____   someone on a low-calorie diet

_____   elderly person with pernicious anemia

_____   alcoholic

_____   someone with multiple food allergies

_____   a child who is a picky eater

✔ Think About It

Ask five classmates about their use of supplements.

1. How many said that they regularly use a supplement? _____

2. What was the primary reason given for using a supplement?

   _____

3. Do you think this is a valid reason? Why or why not?

   _____

4. What foods could you suggest be used instead of a supplement?

   _____

✔ Apply It

Fill in the Nutrition Facts labels for a fruit drink and a 100% real juice product.

Nutrition Facts	
Serving Size	
Servings Per Container	
Amount Per Serving	
Calories	Calories from Fat
	% Daily Value*
Total Fat	
Saturated Fat	
Trans Fat	
Cholesterol	
Sodium	
Total Carbohydrate	
Dietary Fiber	
Sugars	
Protein	
Vitamin A • Vitamin C	
Calcium • Iron • Vitamin D	
* Percent Daily Values are based on a 2,000 calorie diet. Your daily values may be higher or lower depending on your calorie needs:	

Nutrition Facts	
Serving Size	
Servings Per Container	
Amount Per Serving	
Calories	Calories from Fat
	% Daily Value*
Total Fat	
Saturated Fat	
Trans Fat	
Cholesterol	
Sodium	
Total Carbohydrate	
Dietary Fiber	
Sugars	
Protein	
Vitamin A • Vitamin C	
Calcium • Iron • Vitamin D	
* Percent Daily Values are based on a 2,000 calorie diet. Your daily values may be higher or lower depending on your calorie needs:	

Product: _____

Product: _____

1. What similarities are there between the two products? _____

2. Which one has the most vitamin C? _____

3. How does the carbohydrate compare per serving? _____

4. Which one has the most sugar? _____

5. Which product would you choose to purchase? Why? _____

✓ Test It

1. The Food and Drug Administration does not require supplements to list _____ on their labels.
   a. net quantity or contents
   b. the ingredients in descending order
   c. cost or price
   d. the name and address of the manufacturer or distributor

2. The U.S. Pharmacopoeia
   a. endorses health claims made by supplement manufacturers.
   b. is a nonprofit organization.
   c. tests supplements to ensure safety.
   d. is a branch of the Food and Drug Administration.

Two Points of View

Can Some Sun Exposure Be a Good Thing?

Read two professionals' opinions on this topic at the end of the chapter in your textbook, then consider the following questions:

1. What do the experts say are the hazards of sun exposure?

_____

_____

2. What are the current recommendations for sun exposure?

_____

_____

3. Does this seem reasonable to you? Do you follow these recommendations?

_____

_____

4. What is related to vitamin D deficiency?

_____

_____

5. Both experts appear to recommend vitamin D supplementation. What do you think of this recommendation?

_____

6. Would you consider taking a vitamin D supplement as a result of reading these Two Points of View? Why or why not?

_____

_____

8

Minerals and Water

What Is Water and Why Is It so Important?

✓ Know It

Match each term to the appropriate description.

_____	1. essential inorganic elements	a. intracellular
_____	2. fluid inside of cells	b. electrolytes
_____	3. fluid outside of cells	c. water
_____	4. fluid between cells	d. minerals
_____	5. charged ions	e. interstitial
_____	6. most abundant body nutrient	f. extracellular

✔ Find It

Circle the person in each pair who would have the highest amount of body water.

1. average adult female *or* average adult male

2. muscular athlete *or* sedentary individual

3. growing child *or* elderly person

4. obese male *or* average male

5. male with 14 percent body fat *or* male with 22 percent body fat

✔ Think About It

A 170-pound athlete was measured at 8 percent body fat. A calculation estimated his body water at 62 percent. How much does this amount of water weigh?

_____

_____

✔ Apply It

Estimate your own percent of body water, given that the average healthy adult is 60 percent water, muscle is approximately 65 percent water, and fat is 10 to 40 percent water. How or why did you make this estimation?

_____

_____

_____

✔ Test It

1. Electrolytes include

   a. folic acid, cobalamin, and biotin.

   b. sodium, potassium, and chloride.

   c. tryptophan, alanine, and creatine.

   d. carbon, nitrogen and hydrogen.

2. The most abundant substance in the body is

   a. protein and muscle tissue.

   b. carbohydrate.

   c. minerals.

   d. water.

What Does Water Do in Your Body?

✔ Know It

Fill in the letters of the terms described below. Then, using the number corresponding to each letter, fill in the phrase.

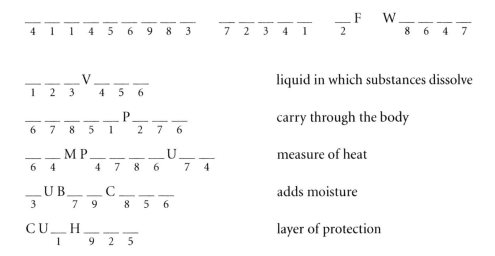

$$\underset{4}{\_}\ \underset{1}{\_}\ \underset{1}{\_}\ \underset{4}{\_}\ \underset{5}{\_}\ \underset{6}{\_}\ \underset{9}{\_}\ \underset{8}{\_}\ \underset{3}{\_} \quad \underset{7}{\_}\ \underset{2}{\_}\ \underset{3}{\_}\ \underset{4}{\_}\ \underset{1}{\_} \quad \underset{2}{\_}\text{F} \quad \text{W}\underset{8}{\_}\ \underset{6}{\_}\ \underset{4}{\_}\ \underset{7}{\_}$$

$$\underset{1}{\_}\ \underset{2}{\_}\ \underset{3}{\_}\text{V}\underset{4}{\_}\ \underset{5}{\_}\ \underset{6}{\_} \qquad \text{liquid in which substances dissolve}$$

$$\underset{6}{\_}\ \underset{7}{\_}\ \underset{8}{\_}\ \underset{5}{\_}\ \underset{1}{\_}\text{P}\underset{2}{\_}\ \underset{7}{\_}\ \underset{6}{\_} \qquad \text{carry through the body}$$

$$\underset{6}{\_}\ \underset{4}{\_}\text{M P}\underset{4}{\_}\ \underset{7}{\_}\ \underset{8}{\_}\ \underset{6}{\_}\text{U}\underset{7}{\_}\ \underset{4}{\_} \qquad \text{measure of heat}$$

$$\underset{3}{\_}\text{U B}\underset{7}{\_}\ \underset{9}{\_}\text{C}\underset{8}{\_}\ \underset{5}{\_}\ \underset{6}{\_} \qquad \text{adds moisture}$$

$$\text{C U}\underset{1}{\_}\text{H}\underset{9}{\_}\ \underset{2}{\_}\ \underset{5}{\_} \qquad \text{layer of protection}$$

✔ Find It

Check the following examples of water use in the body.

_____   taste and saliva

_____   amniotic fluid around a fetus

_____   evaporation of sweat

_____   pernicious anemia

_____   swelling of a sprained ankle

_____   sunburn

✔ Think About It

You went jogging on a warm humid day. Although you sweated profusely, you did not cool off. Why?

_____

_____

✔ Apply It

List foods you had today in which water was used as a solvent.

_____

_____

✔ Test It

1. Water acts as a solvent in the
    a. joints and eyes.
    b. blood.
    c. amniotic fluid.
    d. maintenance of body temperature.

2. Sweat cools the body when it

   a. forms on the skin.

   b. is extremely humid.

   c. evaporates from the skin.

   d. is generated from the body's core.

What Is Water Balance and How Do You Maintain It?

✓ Know It

Complete the crossword puzzle.

Across

2   not enough water in the body

7   hormone that directs volume of water in kidneys

8   water lost daily through respiration and off skin

Down

1   too little sodium in blood

3   movement of a solvent

4   signal to drink

5   water in equals water out

6   cause water to be lost from the body

✔ Find It

*Label each of the following using **I** if the description is a way water enters the body. Use **O** if the description is a way water leaves the body.*

_____ juice   _____ sweat

_____ kidneys, urine   _____ coffee, tea

_____ oatmeal, bread   _____ lungs

_____ large intestine   _____ energy metabolism

✔ Think About It

You and a few friends joined a weight-maintenance group for which you weigh in weekly. One of your friends has advised you to not eat anything salty as well as to limit your beverages the day before you weigh in. What do you think of this advice?

_____

_____

✔ Apply It

1. Weigh yourself before you exercise. _____

2. Weigh yourself immediately after exercise. _____

3. What is the difference between your pre- and postexercise weight? _____

4. Did you drink anything during exercise? _____

5. Did you experience any symptoms of dehydration? _____

✔ Test It

1. The movement of water across cell membranes is

   a. osmosis.

   b. dehydration.

   c. balance.

   d. thirst.

2. _____ cause(s) water loss from the body.

   a. Thirst

   b. Dehydration

   c. Osmosis

   d. Diuretics

How Much Water Do You Need and What Are the Best Sources?

✔ Know It

Match each term to the appropriate description.

_____   1. underground source with naturally occurring minerals   a. spring

_____   2. underground water that flows naturally to the surface   b. vitamin

_____   3. water with carbon dioxide added   c. mineral

_____   4. processed and boiled water   d. distilled

_____   5. water with flavor added; may have added sugars and calories e. sparkling

_____   6. water with vitamins added   f. flavored

✔ Find It

Circle the item that has the most water in each group.

1. bagel *or* cooked rice *or* cooked oatmeal

2. grapes *or* fruit juice *or* banana

3. yogurt *or* milk *or* ice cream

4. eggs *or* beef *or* chicken

✔ Think About It

You have enjoyed two cups of coffee at breakfast every day for the past three years. A friend is certain that this is not a healthy habit for you. One of the reasons she gives is that caffeine is a diuretic and therefore you become dehydrated by drinking coffee. What do you think? Do you need to change your breakfast habit?

_____

_____

✔ Apply It

1. Keep track of the amount of beverages that you take in for one day.

_____

_____

2. How close are you to the recommendation of 9 cups for women or 13 cups for men?

_____

_____

3. What changes do you need to make?

_____

_____

✔ Test It

1. _____ water does not have to adhere to FDA regulations for bottled water.
   a. Spring
   b. Sparkling
   c. Flavored
   d. Vitamin

2. About _____ of your daily water intake can come from foods.

   a. 10 percent

   b. 20 percent

   c. 30 percent

   d. 40 percent

What Are Minerals and Why Do You Need Them?

✔ Know It

Circle the correct term of the choices given in the following sentences.

1. (Organic *or* Inorganic) compounds contain carbon and are formed by living things.

2. Compounds that do not contain carbon are (organic *or* inorganic).

3. Nutrients are absorbed by the body based on the (water content *or* bioavailability) of the food.

4. Sodium, potassium, and sulfur are examples of (major *or* trace) minerals.

5. Iron, zinc, and copper are examples of (major *or* trace) minerals.

✔ Find It

*Use **M** to identify major minerals. Use **T** to identify trace minerals.*

iron	copper	sodium
zinc	chromium	sulfur
chloride	manganese	selenium
potassium	magnesium	phosphorus
calcium	fluoride	nickel

Now circle the mineral that occurs in greatest quantity in the body.

✔ Think About It

1. A label on a supplement gives this information: 20 milligrams iron, 40 milligrams zinc, 25 milligrams chromium, and 400 milligrams calcium. What do you think of this supplement?

    _____

    _____

2. Would you consider using it? Why or why not?

    _____

    _____

✔ Apply It

1. Find a bottle of mineral water at the store. List the minerals that are in this product.

    _____

2. Do you think this is a significant amount of any mineral?

    _____

✔ Test It

1. Calcium, _____, and _____ work to strengthen bones and teeth.
    a. potassium; chloride
    b. iron; zinc
    c. copper; fluoride
    d. phosphorus; magnesium

2. Minerals are found in
    a. water.
    b. plant foods.
    c. animal foods.
    d. all of the above.

Sodium

✔ Know It

Use these terms to complete the sentences.

preservative   natural sources   fluid balance   processed foods

hypertension   electrolyte   flavor

1. Sodium is a(n) _____.

2. Sodium's chief role is regulation of _____.

3. Salt is added to foods to enhance _____.

4. It can also act as a _____.

5. The majority of sodium in the American diet is from _____.

6. About 12 percent of Americans' consumption of sodium is from _____.

7. There is a relationship between sodium intake and _____.

✔ Find It

Pick the food in each group with the most sodium.

1. bread *or* pretzels *or* cornflakes

2. tomato *or* green beans *or* tomato juice

3. pickle *or* apple *or* applesauce

4. chicken *or* turkey *or* hot dog

5. cottage cheese *or* pineapple *or* sunflower seeds

✔ Think About It

A recipe for bread calls for shortening, water, sugar, salt, yeast, and flour. What purposes does salt serve in this recipe?

_____

_____

✔ Apply It

Compare the labels of at least five packaged food items in your cupboard.

Food Item	Serving Size	Sodium, mg

1. What item had the most sodium per serving?

_____

2. What item had the least sodium per serving?

_____

3. Summarize the sodium content of packaged foods that you have on hand.

_____

✔ Test It

1. Acclimation to environmental heat means
    a. less sodium will be lost through sweat.
    b. more sodium will be lost through sweat.
    c. less sodium will be excreted in the urine.
    d. more sodium will be excreted in the urine.

2. Sodium deficiency is _____ in _____.

    a. always found; endurance athletes

    b. rare; healthy individuals

    c. common; elderly individuals

    d. a side effect; hypertension

You and Your Blood Pressure

✔ Know It

Circle the correct answer of the choices given in the following sentences.

1. High blood pressure is known as (hyperthermia *or* hypertension).

2. High blood pressure (decreases *or* increases) the risk of heart disease, stroke, and kidney disease.

3. The force of blood against the artery walls when the heart beats is (systolic *or* diastolic) pressure.

4. The pressure of blood against the artery walls when the heart is at rest between beats is (systolic *or* diastolic) pressure.

5. Hypertension is referred to as the (deadly *or* silent) killer because there are no outward symptoms.

✔ Find It

*Use **C** to identify hypertension risk factors that you can control. Use **X** for risk factors that you cannot control.*

_____	family history	_____	race
_____	age	_____	gender
_____	physical activity	_____	body weight
_____	alcohol intake	_____	sodium intake
_____	stress		

✔ Think About It

You know that your friend's father is on medication for hypertension. He says that he doesn't need to pay much attention to his condition because the medication takes care of everything. What do you think of this reasoning? What behaviors should your friend's father adopt?

_____

_____

✔ Apply It

Keep track of your food intake for one day. Complete the chart to compare your intake to the DASH diet recommendations.

Food Group	DASH	Your Intake
Whole grains	7–8 servings	
Low-fat dairy	2–3 servings	
Fruit	3–4 servings	
Vegetable	3–5 servings	
Lean meat	<4 oz	

1. How does your intake compare to the DASH diet? _____

2. What changes will you make? _____

✔ Test It

1. The DASH diet is
    a. low in calories.
    b. high in lean meat.
    c. high in fruits and vegetables.
    d. low in minerals.

2. To help control blood pressure, alcohol
   a. should be eliminated.
   b. should be consumed daily in the form of wine.
   c. does not have any effect.
   d. should be limited to 1 to 2 drinks per day.

Potassium

✔ Know It

Unscramble the terms to find out the functions of potassium.

1. DUIFL AALBCEN   _____

2. DOBLO FEBFRU   _____

3. CLSMUE TTINOACNROC   _____

4. NVERE UNOCCONDTI   _____

5. DOBLO SEPSREUR   _____

6. NEBO AEHTLH   _____

✔ Find It

Check all of the following that are sources of potassium.

_____ banana   _____ tomato

_____ milk   _____ hamburger

_____ potato   _____ kidney beans

✔ Think About It

Because your grandmother is on an antihypertensive drug, she has been advised to eat good sources of potassium daily. She found a potassium supplement at the store and is now taking it to guarantee potassium intake. What do you think of this practice? What condition could your grandmother risk developing?

_____

_____

_____

✔ Apply It

Add foods to increase potassium.

1, toast + _____

2. turkey, cheese + _____

3. Cheerios, nuts + _____

4. lettuce + _____

✔ Test It

1. A deficiency of potassium is termed
    a. hyperkalemia.
    b. hypokalemia.
    c. hypertension.
    d. hypotension.

2. Hyperkalemia can be caused by
    a. consuming supplements with potassium.
    b. drinking too much orange juice.
    c. anorexia.
    d. chronic diarrhea.

Calcium

✓ Know It

Use these terms to complete the sentences. Terms may be used more than once.

> blood pressure   other tissues   teeth   bones   hypercalcemia
>
> kidney stones   cancer   muscles   obesity   osteoporosis

1. Over 99 percent of the body's calcium is located in _____ and _____.

2. Calcium makes up almost 40 percent of the weight of _____.

3. The remaining 1 percent of calcium is in your _____, _____, and _____.

4. Calcium may reduce _____, _____, _____, and _____.

5. A deficiency of calcium can lead to _____.

6. Too much calcium is referred to as _____.

✓ Find It

Check all of the following that provide calcium.

_____	pork loin	_____	bok choy
_____	yogurt	_____	tofu
_____	applesauce	_____	carrots
_____	cottage cheese	_____	broccoli

✓ Think About It

Outline considerations that you would make prior to choosing or using a calcium supplement.

_____

_____

✔ Apply It

Add food items to increase calcium.

1. cereal + _____

2. pineapple + _____

3. turkey, bread + _____

4. iceberg lettuce + _____

✔ Test It

1. Hypercalcemia can lead to
   a. constipation.
   b. increased absorption of iron and zinc.
   c. osteoporosis.
   d. brittle bones.

2. Calcium may
   a. increase high blood pressure.
   b. increase risk of kidney stones.
   c. reduce risk of obesity.
   d. reduce risk of hypercalcemia.

Phosphorus

✔ Know It

Check all correct choices under each phrase.

1. Phosphorus is

   _____ a major mineral.

   _____ mostly in bones.

   _____ mostly in body fluids.

2. Phosphorus is needed for

_____ bones and teeth.

_____ cell membranes.

_____ energy metabolism.

_____ genetic material.

_____ immunity.

3. Too much dietary phosphorus (is)

_____ termed hyperphosphatemia.

_____ a problem for people with kidney disease.

_____ leads to bone loss.

_____ common.

✔ Find It

Check all of the following that provide phosphorus.

_____ chicken   _____ peas

_____ orange juice   _____ water

_____ milk   _____ strawberries

_____ broccoli   _____ cereal

Now circle the food item above that has the most phosphorus per serving.

✔ Think About It

A public school official has stated that "the phosphorus found in soda pops is leading to school-aged children developing weak bones." What do you think of this statement? How might this statement be clarified?

_____

_____

✓ Apply It

Add foods to increase phosphorus.

1. whole-wheat bread + _____

2. ice cream + _____

3. banana + _____

4. baked potato + _____

✓ Test It

1. A phosphorus deficiency is
   a. referred to as hyperphosphatemia.
   b. common in adolescents.
   c. rare.
   d. seen in individuals with kidney disease.

2. Phosphorus is found in
   a. plant foods.
   b. animal foods.
   c. food additives.
   d. all of the above.

Magnesium

✓ Know It

Check all of the correct choices under each phrase. (Note: There may be more than one correct choice per phrase.)

1. Magnesium is

   _____ a trace mineral.   _____ in intracellular fluid.

   _____ found in bones.   _____ high in blood.

2. Functions of magnesium include

_____ metabolism of energy nutrients.

_____ building healthy muscles.

_____ facilitating nerve function.

_____ maintaining healthy bones.

_____ regulating heart beat.

_____ raising blood pressure.

3. Too much magnesium

_____ occurs with supplement use.

_____ can be a result of food sources.

_____ affects the gastrointestinal tract.

✔ Find It

Check the foods below that provide magnesium.

_____	peanut butter	_____	cottage cheese
_____	chicken	_____	banana
_____	white flour	_____	soda pop
_____	wheat germ	_____	almonds

✔ Think About It

In an effort to lose weight, one of your roommates regularly uses a laxative. What are some of the possible consequences of this behavior?

_____

_____

_____

✔ Apply It

Add food items to increase magnesium.

1. yogurt + _____

2. lettuce + _____

3. salsa + _____

4. whole-grain crackers + _____

✔ Test It

1. Many Americans

    a. take in too much magnesium in the form of laxatives.

    b. don't meet their magnesium needs.

    c. have muscle weakness, depression, and fatigue related to magnesium toxicity.

    d. could benefit from a magnesium supplement.

2. Magnesium is not found in

    a. the bran of grains.

    b. the germ of grains.

    c. refined grains.

    d. animal products.

Chloride and Sulfur

✓ Know It

*Use **Cl** if the phrase describes chloride. Use **S** if the phrase describes sulfur.*

_____   stomach acid   _____   blood buffer

_____   thiamin, biotin, pantothenic acid   _____   amino acids

_____   electrolyte in extracellular fluid   _____   preservative

✓ Find It

Complete the statements using these terms.

        animal food   table salt   3,600 milligrams   not set   plant foods

1. The main source of chloride in the diet is _____.

2. The main source of sulfur in the diet is/are _____.

3. The recommendation for chloride is _____ per day.

4. The recommendation for sulfur is _____.

✓ Think About It

Sodium chloride is 60 percent chloride. If you have 3,500 milligrams of sodium chloride, how many milligrams does the chloride contribute?

_____

✔ Test It

1. Most people
    a. take in a toxic amount of sulfur.
    b. are slightly deficient in sulfur.
    c. could benefit from a sulfur supplement.
    d. get plenty of sulfur in their diet.

2. A chloride deficiency could be seen in someone
    a. who is obese.
    b. following a low-salt diet.
    c. with chronic vomiting or diarrhea.
    d. who avoids fresh fruit.

Osteoporosis: Not Just Your Grandmother's Problem

✔ Know It

Match each term to the appropriate description.

_____ 1. genetically determined maximum amount of bone an individual can build up

_____ 2. amount of minerals per volume in bone

_____ 3. porous, weak, fragile bones at risk for fracture

_____ 4. low bone mass

a. osteoporosis

b. osteopenia

c. peak bone mass

d. bone mineral density

✔ Find It

Check all of the following that are risk factors for osteoporosis.

_____ being male

_____ being Caucasian or Asian-American

_____ being an endurance athlete

_____ adolescence

_____ family history of bone fractures

_____ smoking

_____ limited consumption of alcohol

_____ consuming less than 3 cups of dairy products daily

✔ Think About It

1. Reducing risk of developing osteoporosis would be most beneficial at what age?

   _____

2. Do you think typical college students are at risk of osteopenia?

   _____

3. Why or why not?

   _____

✔ Apply It

Complete the Self-Assessment on pages 284–285 of your textbook. Fill in the skeleton below as directed.

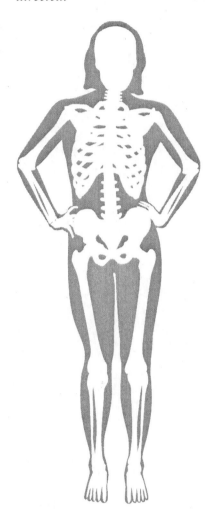

1. What have you learned about your risk for osteoporosis?

   _____

   _____

   _____

2. What lifestyle changes will you make as a result of this self-assessment?

_____

_____

_____

_____

✓ Test It

1. Which statement about osteoporosis is false?
   a. Complications as a result of a hip fracture can lead to death.
   b. Hip fractures are easy to repair.
   c. Hip fractures can affect quality of life.
   d. Osteoporosis is a common condition.

2. Controllable risk factors for osteoporosis include
   a. calcium, exercise, and tobacco use.
   b. family history, alcohol use, and gender.
   c. age, lack of sex hormones, and ethnicity.
   d. body type, gender, and medication use.

Iron

✓ Know It

Match each term to the appropriate description.

_____	1. blood protein	a. nonheme iron
_____	2. iron from animal sources	b. myoglobin
_____	3. iron from plant sources	c. iron-deficiency anemia
_____	4. muscle protein	d. hemoglobin
_____	5. most common nutrient deficiency	e. hemochromatosis
_____	6. genetic disorder causing iron overload	f. heme iron

✔ Find It

*Use **H** to identify heme sources of iron. Use **N** to identify nonheme sources of iron.*

_____   breakfast cereal   _____   tuna fish

_____   raisins   _____   cast-iron cookware

_____   brown sugar, molasses   _____   tofu

_____   sirloin steak   _____   black beans

✔ Think About It

One of your classmates looks pale and often falls asleep in class. She says that even though she sleeps eight hours a night, she can barely drag herself around.

1. What might you suspect?

    _____

2. How could she be certain of a diagnosis?

    _____

3. What are some possible causes?

    _____

    _____

    _____

✔ Apply It

Add foods to increase iron content or iron absorption.

1. eggs + _____

2. milk + _____

3. raisins, almonds + _____

4. baked potato + _____

✔ Test It

1. The most common nutrient deficiency in the United States is
   a. iron-deficiency anemia.
   b. pernicious anemia.
   c. obesity.
   d. calcium.

2. Nonheme sources of iron include
   a. steak, tofu, and shrimp.
   b. breakfast cereal, raisins, and cast-iron cookware.
   c. chicken, spinach, and potatoes.
   d. tuna fish, kidney beans, and turkey.

Copper

✔ Know It

Circle the best term(s) of those given in the following sentences.

1. Copper is part of many (enzymes *or* hormones) and (lipids *or* proteins).

2. Copper is important for (iron *or* calcium) absorption.

3. Copper helps (generate *or* recycle) energy in your cells.

4. Copper plays a role in (bone density *or* blood clotting).

5. Copper deficiency is (rare *or* common) in the United States.

✔ Find It

Check all of the following that contain copper.

_____   walnuts   _____   wheat germ

_____   black beans   _____   hot cocoa

_____   turkey   _____   liver

_____   raisins   _____   oatmeal

Now circle the food item with the highest amount of copper per serving.

✔ Think About It

A child you are babysitting swallows a penny. Do you need to worry about copper toxicity? Why or why not?

_____

_____

_____

✔ Apply It

Add food items to increase copper content.

1. cocoa + _____

2. rice + _____

3. raisins + _____

4. whole-grain pita + _____

✔ Test It

1. Copper deficiency has occurred in
   a. premature babies on formula.
   b. poorly nourished infants fed cow's milk.
   c. individuals on intravenous feedings.
   d. all of the above.

2. Copper plays a role in
   a. bone mineral density.
   b. blood clotting.
   c. hyperkalemia.
   d. cancer prevention.

Zinc

✔ Know It

Check the phrases below that are true of zinc.

_____   needed for protein synthesis

_____   used in energy metabolism

_____   helps produce red blood cells

_____   reduces inflammation of skin wounds

_____   has a role in taste acuity

_____   helps cure the common cold

_____   reduces risk of age-related macular degeneration

_____   vegetarians have a higher need

✓ Find It

Circle the best zinc source in each group.

1. wheat bread *or* wheat germ *or* oatmeal

2. flank steak *or* watermelon *or* mushrooms

3. rice *or* shrimp *or* peas

4. yogurt *or* spinach *or* almonds

✓ Think About It

A vitamin and mineral supplement advertises that it contains "everything from A to zinc." Why would this claim be made?

_____

_____

✓ Apply It

Add food items to increase zinc.

1. crackers + _____

2. oatmeal + _____

3. yogurt + _____

4. pasta + _____

✓ Test It

1. Zinc is
   a. a major mineral.
   b. needed for growth and development.
   c. a cure for the common cold.
   d. an antioxidant.

2. Excessive zinc

    a. can cause delayed sexual maturation.

    b. improves the immune system.

    c. raises HDL cholesterol.

    d. can cause nausea, vomiting, and diarrhea.

Selenium

✔ Know It

Circle the correct answer in the following statements.

1. Selenium is part of a class of (lipids *or* proteins).

2. Selenoproteins act as (enzymes *or* hormones).

3. Selenium is also an (antioxidant *or* energy) nutrient.

4. Selenium may help (cause *or* fight) cancer.

5. A selenium toxicity is called (selenosis *or* Keshar disease).

6. Children who live in rural areas with selenium-poor soil may develop (selenosis *or* Keshar disease).

✔ Find It

Circle the food in each group with the most selenium.

1. green beans *or* pear *or* chicken

2. roast beef *or* cheddar cheese *or* apple

3. broccoli *or* egg *or* wheat crackers

4. banana *or* Brazil nuts *or* walnuts

✔ Think About It

You know that some of your relatives have had various cancers, including colon cancer and prostate cancer. Do you think taking a selenium supplement would be prudent? Why or why not?

_____

_____

✔ Apply It

Add food items to increase selenium.

1. pasta + _____

2. bagel + _____

3. apple + _____

4. almonds + _____

✔ Test It

1. Selenium's _____ properties can potentially slow tumor growth.
    a. hormone
    b. enzyme
    c. antioxidant
    d. protein

2. Selenium prevalence depends on
    a. the amount in the soil where plants are grown.
    b. cooking methods.
    c. storage or refrigeration.
    d. the specific animal source.

Fluoride

✔ Know It

Check the following that are functions of fluoride.

_____ repairs tooth enamel

_____ reduces bacterial acid in the mouth

_____ protects teeth

_____ is a component of saliva

_____ occurs naturally in many foods

_____ interferes with bone development

✔ Find It

Check the phrases that are true of fluorosis.

_____ caused by not enough fluoride

_____ teeth are pitted and mottled

_____ teeth are resistant to decay

_____ infants and children are most at risk

_____ elderly are at high risk

_____ a possible cause is eating toothpaste

✔ Think About It

It is common practice for dentists to treat children's and adolescents' teeth with fluoride. Do you think this is needed if a community has a fluoridated water supply? Why or why not?

_____

_____

_____

✔ Apply It

Find out if your community's water is fluoridated. Check the Centers for Disease Control and Prevention's website: http://apps.need.cdc.gov/MWF/index.asp. What did you find?

_____

_____

_____

✔ Test It

1. Fluoride is commonly found in

    a. fruits.

    b. vegetables.

    c. animal products.

    d. water.

2. Fluorosis occurs

    a. when teeth are forming.

    b. after teeth have erupted through the gums.

    c. when bones calcify.

    d. along with osteoporosis.

Chromium

✔ Know It

Circle the correct answer of the choices given in the following sentences.

1. Chromium is a (trace *or* major) (essential *or* nonessential) mineral.

2. Chromium helps (decrease *or* increase) the effectiveness of insulin.

3. Chromium (has *or* has not) been shown to help build muscle mass.

4. Chromium deficiencies are (common *or* rare) in the United States.

5. The average American eats (adequate *or* inadequate) amounts of chromium.

✔ Find It

Choose the best chromium source in each group.

1. chicken *or* peas *or* milk

2. cottage cheese *or* banana *or* turkey

3. broccoli *or* potato *or* orange juice

4. apple *or* egg *or* cheese

✔ Think About It

One of the personal trainers at the gym is selling chromium picolinate. He says that it has helped him to lose body fat while gaining muscle mass. Are you interested in trying the free samples he offers? Why or why not?

_____

_____

✔ Apply It

Find a chromium supplement at the store.

1. How much chromium is in one serving?

   _____

2. How does that compare with the chromium recommendations for you (30 to 35 micrograms for men, 20 to 25 micrograms for women)?

   _____

3. How does the supplement compare with a cup of broccoli (22 micrograms)?

   _____

4. What can you summarize about the chromium supplement?

   _____

✔ Test It

1. Chromium may have a role in
   a. fat loss.
   b. building lean tissue.
   c. insulin sensitivity.
   d. cancer prevention.

2. _____ are low in chromium.
   a. Grains
   b. Meat, fish, and poultry
   c. Fruits
   d. Dairy products

Iodine

✔ Know It

Match the term to the appropriate description.

_____	1. enlarged thyroid gland	a. congenital
_____	2. low amount of thyroid hormone	b. salt
_____	3. born with	c. hypothyroidism
_____	4. result of iodine deficiency during pregnancy	d. goiter
_____	5. primary source of iodine in the diet	e. cretinism

✔ Find It

Check all of the following that are sources of iodine.

_____ drinking water

_____ kosher salt

_____ milk

_____ pickles

_____ canned soup

_____ cod fish

✔ Think About It

The thyroid needs iodine to make essential hormones. These hormones help to regulate metabolic rate (the rate at which you burn calories). Would additional iodized salt help to promote weight loss? Why or why not?

_____

_____

✓ Apply It

1. Check the salt in your cupboard. Is it iodized?

   _____

2. Check the salt packets in the cafeteria. Is this salt iodized?

   _____

3. Summarize your intake of iodine from salt.

   _____

✓ Test It

1. A goiter is
   a. a sign of iodine deficiency.
   b. due to too much thyroxin.
   c. caused by ingesting too much salt.
   d. a condition common in the Midwest.

2. Thyroid hormones
   a. act as antioxidants.
   b. increase insulin sensitivity.
   c. help decrease LDL cholesterol.
   d. regulate metabolic rate.

Manganese

✓ Know It

Check the phrases below that are true of manganese.

_____   part of hormones

_____   activates many enzymes

_____ involved in metabolism of the energy nutrients

_____ helps bone formation

_____ deficiencies are common

_____ cinnamon is a good source

✔ Find It

Select the best manganese source in the following groups.

1. whole-wheat bread *or* rice *or* raisin bran cereal

2. peas *or* spinach *or* sweet potato

3. pineapple *or* strawberries *or* banana

4. milk *or* lentils *or* pecans

✔ Think About It

The label of a mineral complex supplement states it contains 5 milligrams of manganese per dose. What do you think of this level of manganese? Would you consider using this product? Why or why not?

_____

_____

_____

✔ Apply It

Add food items to increase manganese.

1. whole-wheat toast + _____

2. rice + _____

3. frozen yogurt + _____

4. vegetable soup + _____

✔ Test It

1. Manganese deficiency
   a. causes Parkinson's disease–like symptoms.
   b. is rare.
   c. is common in miners.
   d. affects insulin sensitivity.

2. Manganese is needed
   a. to build muscle mass.
   b. to produce thyroxin.
   c. for bone formation.
   d. to reduce free radicals.

Molybdenum

✔ Know It

Circle the correct answer in the following sentences.

1. Molybdenum is a (trace *or* major) mineral.

2. Molybdenum is involved in the breakdown of (glucose *or* amino acids).

3. Molybdenum is part of several (enzymes *or* hormones).

4. Americans generally consume (adequate *or* inadequate) amounts of molybdenum.

✔ Find It

Check the food sources of molybdenum.

_____ whole-grain bread   _____ broccoli

_____ chickpeas   _____ brown rice

_____ cheddar cheese   _____ lentils

_____ kiwi   _____ garbanzo beans

✔ Test It

1. In animal studies, too much molybdenum caused

   a. Parkinson's disease–like symptoms.

   b. reproductive problems.

   c. rapid heart rate and headaches.

   d. dry skin rashes.

Other Minerals: Arsenic, Boron, Nickel, Silicon, and Vanadium

✔ Know It

Match each mineral to the appropriate potential role and/or disease symptom.

_____ 1. considered essential in animals; needed by specific enzymes	a. arsenic
_____ 2. insulin-like actions	b. boron
_____ 3. deficiency associated with reproduction abnormalities in fish and frogs	c. nickel
_____ 4. deficiency may impair growth and reproduction in animals	d. silicon
_____ 5. may be needed for bone formation	e. vanadium

✔ Find It

Using the minerals from **Know It** *(on the previous page), match each to the food sources listed below.*

_____ dairy products

_____ meat, poultry

_____ grain products

_____ nuts, legumes

_____ vegetables

_____ parsley and black pepper

✔ Think About It

Do you expect to see the trace minerals from **Know It** (on the previous page) listed on food packages? Why or why not?

_____

_____

✔ Test It

1. Arsenic can be found in

    a. meat and dairy products.

    b. nuts and legumes.

    c. grain products.

    d. fruits and vegetables.

2. A deficiency of _____ may be associated with reproduction abnormalities in fish and frogs.

    a. arsenic

    b. boron

    c. silicon

    d. nickel

Two Points of View

Shaking the Habit

Read two professionals' opinions on this topic at the end of the chapter in your textbook, then consider the following questions:

1. According to the experts, is the DRI of 1,500 milligrams of sodium an achievable goal for most Americans?

   _____

   _____

2. Are there some people who need more sodium than this? Who and why?

   _____

   _____

3. Do typical college students need to restrict their sodium intake? Why or why not?

   _____

4. List the key components of the DASH diet.

   _____

   _____

5. What steps can you take to implement components of the DASH diet?

   _____

   _____

9
Alcohol

What Is Alcohol and How Is It Made?

✓ Know It

Match each term to the appropriate description.

_____	1.	alcohol used for human consumption	a.	fermentation
_____	2.	compound used in antifreeze	b.	liquor
_____	3.	compound used in rubbing alcohol	c.	distillation
_____	4.	process of yeast breaking down sugar	d.	ethanol
_____	5.	process of heating and vaporizing alcohol	e.	isopropanol
_____	6.	concentrated product of distilling	f.	methanol

✔ Find It

Check the phrases that are true of alcohol.

_____   essential nutrient

_____   contains food energy

_____   legally sold in the United States

_____   expensive compared with bottled water

_____   can be toxic

_____   beer is made from grains

_____   wine is made from grains

✔ Think About It

What basic supplies would be needed to make ethanol?

_____

_____

_____

✔ Apply It

List common uses for various types of alcohol.

_____

_____

_____

✓ Test It

1. Methanol is
   a. made from fermented grapes.
   b. used as an antiseptic.
   c. safe in moderation.
   d. used in antifreeze.

2. Alcohol
   a. is nutrient dense.
   b. is carbohydrate rich.
   c. can be toxic.
   d. is an inexpensive beverage.

Why Do People Drink Alcohol?

✓ Know It

Check the reasons why people choose to drink alcohol.

_____ celebration

_____ relaxation

_____ sleep aid

_____ pleasure

_____ escape reality

_____ religious tradition

_____ appetite suppressant

_____ habit

✔ Find It

*Use **W** to identify what would be considered moderate alcohol consumption for women; use **M** for men.*

_____   22 ounces tall tap beer

_____   2 ounces tequila

_____   4 ounces Chablis wine

_____   12 ounces hard lemonade

_____   1 ounce apricot brandy

✔ Think About It

People in France have a lower rate of heart disease than Americans. If you decide to study abroad in France next year, will your risk of heart disease decrease? Why or why not?

_____

_____

✔ Apply It

Determine the alcohol habits of five classmates.

Name	Number of Times per Week Uses Alcohol	Number of Drinks per Session	Type of Alcohol	Abstains

What did you learn that surprised you?

_____

✔ Test It

1. Alcohol may offer heart health benefits to

   a. people who drink red wine.

   b. women aged 55 and over.

   c. anyone over 21.

   d. men aged 60 and over.

2. Alcohol is classified as a

   a. supplement.

   b. nutrient.

   c. drug.

   d. poison.

What Happens to Alcohol in the Body?

✔ Know It

Circle the correct answer of the choices given in the following sentences.

1. Your body (can *or* cannot) store alcohol.

2. (Twenty *or* eighty) percent of alcohol is absorbed through the stomach.

3. The majority of alcohol is absorbed in the (stomach *or* small intestine).

4. Women have (less *or* more) alcohol dehydrogenase in their stomach than men.

5. (Muscular *or* Obese) individuals are able to distribute more alcohol throughout their bodies than

   those who have (more *or* less) fat tissue.

6. Alcohol is primarily metabolized in the (blood *or* liver).

7. The amount of alcohol in your breath (correlates *or* does not correlate) with the amount of alcohol

   in your blood.

8. Alcohol is a central nervous system (stimulant *or* depressant).

✔ Find It

Select the person in each pair more likely to metabolize alcohol slower.

1. female eating a salad *or* female eating a cheeseburger

2. 20-year-old female *or* 18-year-old male

3. 160-pound male *or* 158-pound female

4. a couch potato *or* an athlete

5. student who skipped lunch *or* student who had pizza for lunch

✔ Think About It

1. Your friend told you that the sure cure for a hangover is tomato juice with Tabasco sauce. What do you think of this cure?

   _____

   _____

   _____

2. If you fell asleep drunk, could you still be intoxicated when you wake up in the morning?

   _____

   _____

   _____

✓ Apply It

Table 9.1

Blood Alcohol Concentration Tables

For Women
Body Weight in Pounds

Drinks per hour	100	120	140	160	180	200
1	0.05	0.04	0.03	0.03	0.03	0.02
2	0.09	0.08	0.07	0.06	0.05	0.05
3	0.14	0.11	0.10	0.09	0.08	0.07
4	0.18	0.15	0.13	0.11	0.10	0.09
5	0.23	0.19	0.16	0.14	0.13	0.11
6	0.27	0.23	0.19	0.17	0.15	0.14
7	0.32	0.27	0.23	0.20	0.18	0.16
8	0.36	0.30	0.26	0.23	0.20	0.18
9	0.41	0.34	0.29	0.26	0.30	0.20
10	0.45	0.38	0.32	0.28	0.25	0.23

For Men
Body Weight in Pounds

Drinks per hour	100	120	140	160	180	200
1	0.04	0.03	0.03	0.02	0.02	0.02
2	0.08	0.06	0.05	0.05	0.04	0.04
3	0.11	0.09	0.08	0.07	0.06	0.06
4	0.15	0.12	0.11	0.09	0.08	0.08
5	0.19	0.16	0.13	0.12	0.11	0.09
6	0.23	0.19	0.16	0.14	0.13	0.11
7	0.26	0.22	0.19	0.16	0.15	0.13
8	0.30	0.25	0.21	0.19	0.17	0.15
9	0.34	0.28	0.24	0.21	0.19	0.17
10	0.38	0.31	0.27	0.23	0.21	0.19

Notes: Shaded area indicates legal intoxication.
Blood alcohol concentrations are expressed as percent, meaning grams of alcohol per 10 milliliters (per deciliter) of blood. Tables are adapted from those of the Pennsylvania Liquor Control Board, Harrisburg.

1. Using the chart above, how many drinks can you have to feel relaxed (BAC 0.01 to 0.05)?

   _____

2. What will your BAC be after having three drinks in an hour? _____

3. If the legal BAC for driving is 0.08, how much can you drink before reaching that level?

   _____

✓ Test It

1. The enzyme alcohol dehydrogenase
   a. is higher in women than in men.
   b. is found in the blood.
   c. works to metabolize alcohol in the stomach.
   d. speeds up alcohol absorption in the blood.

2. Having a few beers with dinner means
   a. the alcohol will not be absorbed.
   b. the absorption of alcohol will be delayed.
   c. intoxication is not possible.
   d. the fat calories will not be absorbed.

How Can Alcohol Be Harmful?

✓ Know It

Complete the crossword puzzle.

Across

3 symptoms resulting from excessive alcohol intake
4 fetal alcohol spectrum disorders
5 fetal alcohol syndrome
7 inflammation of the stomach
8 only cure for a hangover
10 step 3 of alcohol liver disease
11 damaging product produced by intestinal bacteria
12 enhance taste

Down

1 step 2 of alcohol liver disease
2 poor nutrition
6 step 1 of alcohol liver disease
9 alcohol associated with male and female sexual dysfunction

✔ Find It

Unscramble the letters to form words that list harmful effects of alcohol.

1. REGNHAVO   _____

2. EURDICTI   _____

3. RLTYCLEELETO LAAMECIBN   _____   _____

4. SOOSESOTROIP   _____

5. RECCNA   _____

6. NUNRITET PSARBONITO   _____   _____

7. EVILR AEDEISS   _____   _____

✔ Think About It

1. If you drink moderate amounts of caffeine, over time it no longer acts as a diuretic. If you drink enough alcohol, can you overcome its diuretic effect?

   _____

   _____

2. Does the same amount of alcohol continue to have the same effect over time? Why or why not?

   _____

   _____

   _____

   _____

✔ Apply It

1. Look at your school newspaper. How many advertisements can you find that feature alcohol in a glamorous way?

    _____

2. Does your school have a policy against alcohol advertising?

    _____

3. How many hallway posters can you find that glamorize alcohol consumption?

    _____

4. Are there any advertisements that promote responsible use of alcohol?

    _____

5. How have these advertisements affected you?

    _____

    _____

✔ Test It

1. Treat a hangover with
    a. an alcoholic beverage.
    b. orange juice and/or coffee.
    c. nonsteroidal anti-inflammatory medication.
    d. time.

2. The leading cause of mental retardation and birth defects is
    a. cirrhosis of the liver.
    b. malnutrition.
    c. fetal alcohol syndrome.
    d. unintentional injuries.

What Are Alcohol Abuse and Alcoholism?

✓ Know It

Match the term with the appropriate description.

_____ 1. continuation of alcohol consumption even though it has become a destructive behavior

_____ 2. craving alcohol, can't control intake; abstaining will cause withdrawal symptoms

_____ 3. chronic disease with genetic, psychological, and environmental components

_____ 4. four to five drinks in a short time period

_____ 5. when an intoxicated person cannot recall an event

_____ 6. BAC at an extreme level; central nervous system is affected

_____ 7. body adjusts to long-term alcohol use

a. alcoholism

b. dependence

c. tolerance

d. alcohol abuse

e. poisoning

f. blackout

g. binge

✓ Find It

Check the classic symptoms of alcoholism.

_____ needs more alcohol for it to have an effect

_____ craves salty foods along with alcohol

_____ has symptoms of withdrawal if alcohol intake is halted

_____ craves alcohol

_____ can control and limit intake

_____ cannot control or limit intake

_____ family history of alcoholism

✓ Think About It

One of your roommates shows all of the classic symptoms of alcoholism. In addition, she has started to skip classes and miss work. You are concerned about her.

1. What can you do to help her?

   _____

   _____

2. What if she denies her disease and becomes defensive?

   _____

   _____

3. What could help you understand your roommate's behavior?

   _____

   _____

✓ Apply It

Self-Assessment

Red Flags for Alcohol Abuse

Complete the following self-assessment to see if you may be at increased risk for alcohol abuse.

1. Do you fail to fulfill major work, school, or home responsibilities because of your consumption of alcohol?   **Yes** ☐   **No** ☐

2. Do you drink in situations that are potentially dangerous, such as while driving a car or operating heavy machinery?   **Yes** ☐   **No** ☐

3. Do you experience repeated alcohol-related legal problems, such as being arrested for driving while intoxicated?   **Yes** ☐   **No** ☐

4. Do you have relationship problems that are caused or made worse by alcohol?   **Yes** ☐   **No** ☐

Answers

If you answered yes to any of these questions, you should speak with your health care provider for insight and guidance.

Source: Adapted from National Institute on Alcohol Abuse and Alcoholism. 2003. Understanding alcohol: Investigations into Biology and Behavior. Available at http://science.education.nih.gov/supplements/nih3/alcohol/default.htm. Accessed December 2005; U.S. Department of Health and Human Services. 1997. Ninth Special Report of the U.S. Congress on Alcohol and Health. Bethesda, MD: National Institute on Alcohol Abuse and Alcoholism.

What changes do you need to make in your behavior around alcohol?

_____

_____

✔ Test It

1. Increased alcohol intake is associated with

    a. isolation.

    b. joining groups (such as fraternities and sororities).

    c. postcollege years.

    d. becoming an adult of legal age.

2. The _____ in life a person starts drinking, the _____ the chances that alcohol will become a problem later in life.

    a. later; higher

    b. earlier; lower

    c. earlier; higher

    d. Chances that alcohol will become a problem later in life are the same no matter when a person starts drinking.

Who Should Avoid Alcohol and What Is Moderate Drinking?

✔ Know It

Check the following people who should abstain from alcohol.

_____ pregnant or lactating women

_____ college students

_____ children

_____ elderly people

_____ those taking over-the-counter medications

_____ those taking prescription medications

_____ operators of heavy equipment

_____ school bus drivers

_____ department store clerks

✔ Find It

Check the following that are a standard drink (¹/₂ ounce alcohol).

_____   12 ounces brewed beer

_____   16 ounces tap beer

_____   22 ounces imported beer

_____   12 ounces light beer

_____   5 ounces red wine

_____   8 ounces white wine

✔ Think About It

One of your friends parties hard on the weekend, but avoids alcohol the rest of the week. Your friend considers himself a moderate drinker. Is this behavior an example of moderation? What can you tell your friend about his drinking pattern?

_____

_____

✔ Apply It

Determine your own drinking behavior.

1. Number of times per week that you have alcohol: _____

2. Number of drinks during that time: _____

3. Do you abstain from alcohol use? _____

4. Are you a moderate drinker, binge drinker, or other? _____

✓ Test It

1. Those who can use alcohol in moderation include

    a. women of childbearing age who may become pregnant.

    b. people using over-the-counter medications.

    c. those with a built-up tolerance.

    d. college students of legal drinking age.

2. As a moderate drinker, you need to watch out for the _____ and the _____.

    a. time of the evening; amount of food consumed

    b. size of your drinks; frequency of your drinking

    c. amount your friends drink; availability of a cab

    d. day of the week; time you work in the morning

Two Points of View

Are There Health Benefits to Drinking Alcohol?

Read two professionals' opinions on this topic at the end of the chapter in your textbook, then consider the following questions:

1. According to David Anderson, PhD, what are some of the possible health benefits of drinking alcohol?

    _____

    _____

2. What are some of the possible negative consequences?

    _____

    _____

3. According to Charles Bamforth, PhD, what are some of the possible health benefits of drinking alcohol?

    _____

    _____

4. What are some of the possible negative consequences?

    _____

    _____

5. What has the College Alcohol Survey shown?

    _____

    _____

6. What other research has been done on alcohol and disease?

    _____

    _____

7. Do you think either expert's affiliations affected his answers to the questions posed in **Two Points of View**? If so, how?

    _____

    _____

10 Weight Management

What Is Weight Management and Why Is It Important?

✓ Know It

Match each term to the appropriate definition.

_____ 1. having an unhealthy amount of body fat   a. underweight

_____ 2. weighing too little for your height   b. weight management

_____ 3. body weight for height without risk of chronic disease   c. overweight

_____ 4. maintaining body weight   d. obesity

_____ 5. weighing 10 to 15 pounds more than healthy weight for height   e. healthy weight

✔ Find It

Check all of the following that are health-related risks of being overweight.

_____ heart disease

_____ type 2 diabetes

_____ wrinkled skin

_____ arthritis

_____ sleep apnea

_____ excess body hair

_____ some cancers

✔ Think About It

When you're home for a weekend, you see a high school friend. She appears to have lost a lot of weight since you last saw her six months ago. What could be possible causes of her weight loss?

_____

_____

✔ Apply It

Look through a few popular lifestyle magazines for ads of weight-loss products or techniques. Do a magazine comparison of advertisements using the table below.

Magazine Name	Number of Advertisements for Weight-Loss Products	Number of Articles on Weight Maintenance	Number of Advertisements for High-Calorie Food Items	Number of Articles on Cooking and/or Recipes

1. From your brief study, how many advertisements for weight-loss products were in a typical

    magazine? _____

2. On average, how many articles focused on weight maintenance? _____

3. Were there recipes or advertisements for high-calorie food items? _____

4. How can you summarize your study?

    _____

    _____

    _____

✔ Test It

1. As a person's weight increases, his or her
    a. blood pressure decreases.
    b. blood pressure increases.
    c. risk of gallbladder disease decreases.
    d. HDL increases.

2. Weighing 10 to 15 pounds more than a healthy weight for your height is termed
    a. weight management.
    b. obesity.
    c. overweight.
    d. malnutrition.

How Do You Know if You're at a Healthy Weight?

✓ Know It

Complete the crossword puzzle.

Across
1   fat stored beneath the skin
4   estimating body fat using an electrical current
6   fat stored in the abdominal area
7   relationship of weight to height
8   estimating body fat through water displacement

Down
1   estimating body fat using calipers to measure skin thickness at designated sites
2   equipment used to measure air displacement
3   a beam of energy is used to measure bone, fat, and lean tissue
5   obesity due to excess visceral fat

✔ Find It

Check all of the following methods that measure percent of body fat.

_____ BMI

_____ skinfold thickness

_____ bioelectrical impedance

_____ bathroom scale

_____ underwater weighing

_____ BodPod

_____ dual X-ray absorptiometry

Now circle the techniques that are direct measures of body fat.

✔ Think About It

A football linebacker at your school is under coach's orders to put on 30 pounds of additional bulk over the summer. You calculated his BMI at 32. Do you think this football player is at risk for health-related consequences due to the planned weight increase? Why or why not?

_____

_____

_____

_____

✓ Apply It

Calculate your body mass index (BMI).

$$BMI = \frac{weight\ (pounds) \times 703}{height\ squared\ (inches^2)} = \underline{\hspace{4cm}}$$

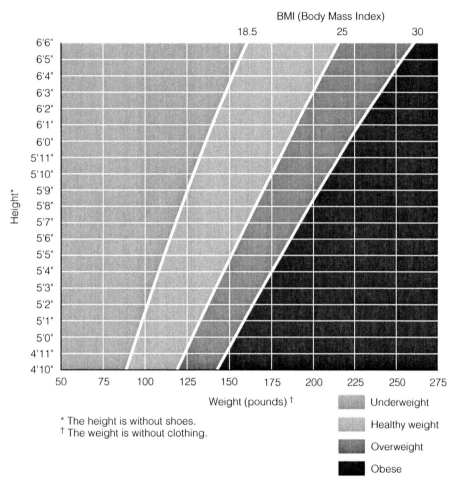

* The height is without shoes.
† The weight is without clothing.

(Refer to page 341 in your textbook for a full-color version of this image.)

1. What range are you in according to the BMI chart?

_____

2. Do you think this is an accurate assessment for you? Why?

_____

_____

_____

✓ Test It

1. Central obesity is due to storing too much
    a. subcutaneous fat.
    b. visceral fat.
    c. BMI.
    d. beer.

2. Body mass index is a
    a. measure of body fatness.
    b. direct measure of ideal body weight.
    c. relationship of weight to height.
    d. measure of central obesity.

What Is Energy Balance and What Determines Energy Needs?

✓ Know It

Match each term to the appropriate description.

_____ 1. energy intake equals energy output

_____ 2. store more energy than expended

_____ 3. expend more energy than consumed

_____ 4. energy needed to meet basic needs

_____ 5. metabolically active body tissue

_____ 6. calories used for digestion

_____ 7. calories needed to maintain energy balance

a. negative energy balance

b. basal metabolic rate

c. energy balance

d. estimated energy requirement

e. thermic effect of food

f. positive energy balance

g. lean body mass

✓ Find It

1. Circle the factor that will increase basal metabolic rate.

   a. muscle mass *or* fat tissue

   b. infant *or* adult

   c. woman *or* man

   d. short individual *or* tall individual

   e. Caucasian *or* African-American

   f. fever/illness *or* wellness

   g. feasting *or* fasting

   h. lemonade *or* espresso coffee

   i. hot environment *or* cold environment

2. Which pair of factors affects BMI equally?

_____

✓ Think About It

In an effort to lose weight, one of your friends has turned down the heat in her apartment so that she shivers. She has also started to smoke.

1. What can you tell her about these techniques?

_____

_____

2. What might help her to be successful with weight maintenance?

_____

_____

✔ Apply It

Complete this self-assessment to determine your EER.

What's Your Estimated Energy Expenditure (EER)?

Calculating your EER is a two-step process.

1. First, complete the information below.

   a. My age is ☐

   b. My physical activity during the day based on the chart below is ☐

Physical Activity	Male	Female
Sedentary (no exercise)	1.00	1.00
Low active (walks about 2 miles daily at 3–4 mph)	1.11	1.12
Active (walks about 7 miles daily at 3–4 mph)	1.26	1.27
Very active (walks about 17 miles daily at 3–4 mph)	1.48	1.45

   c. My weight in pounds is _____ divided by 2.2 = ☐ kg

   d. My height in inches is _____ divided by 39.4 = ☐ meters

2. Using your answers in each box in step 1, complete the following calculation based on your gender and age.

   Males, 19+ years old, use this calculation:

   662 − (9.53 × _____) + _____ × (15.91 × _____ + 539.6 × _____)
              a   **b**   **c**   **d**

   = _____
      EER

   Females, 19+ years old, use this calculation:

   354 − (6.91 × _____) + _____ × (9.36 × _____ + 726 × _____)
              a   **b**   **c**   **d**

   = _____
      EER

✔ Test It

1. The factor that lowers basal metabolic rate is

   a. going to a hot environment.

   b. going to a cold environment.

   c. becoming pregnant.

   d. starvation.

2. The TEF for an average person who eats three meals a day is about _____ of total energy needs.

   a. 10 percent

   b. 20 to 35 percent

   c. 50 to 70 percent

   d. 80 to 100 percent

What Are the Effects of an Energy Imbalance?

✔ Know It

*Look at the following scenarios. Use a **P** to identify a behavior that would lead to positive energy balance. Use an **N** to identify negative energy balance.*

_____ going to coffee break every day and consuming a doughnut

_____ stopping on the way to class for a mocha latté

_____ walking instead of driving to work

_____ skipping breakfast and lunch

_____ drinking three beers every evening

_____ eating only fruit

✔ Find It

Select the lower calorie option in each pair.

1. pretzels *or* potato chips

2. doughnut *or* bagel

3. iced tea *or* soda pop

4. carrots *or* french fries

5. brownie *or* fruit cocktail

✔ Think About It

You start a job at a local restaurant. One of the benefits of the job is being able to eat a meal free during your shift. Even though you are busy on the job, after the first month you notice that your pants feel too tight. What could be to blame for this?

_____

_____

_____

✔ Apply It

List snack foods that you like to consume. List the calories per serving. Calculate the number of servings it would take to add up to an extra pound of body fat (3,500 calories).

Food Item	Calories per Serving	Number of Servings to Equal 3,500 Calories

What changes do you need to make in your snacking choices or habits?

_____

_____

_____

✓ Test It

1. The body has unlimited ability to store
   a. carbohydrate.
   b. glucose.
   c. protein.
   d. fat.

2. One hundred extra calories a day is equal to a pound in
   a. a year.
   b. a semester.
   c. a month.
   d. three months.

What Factors Are Likely to Affect Body Weight?

✓ Know It

Unscramble the letters to spell each term described.

sensation of eating enough	AEITTYS
	_ _ _ _ _ _ _
hormone that increases hunger	RLNIHEG
	_ _ _ _ _ _ _
hormone produced in fat	INELTP
	_ _ _ _ _ _
hormone released when the stomach is distended	KCSELIINCYHNOTO
	_ _ _ _ _ _ _ _ _ _ _ _ _ _ _
production of heat	EMGESHRETSONSI
	_ _ _ _ _ _ _ _ _ _ _ _ _ _

✓ Find It

Check the activities that are examples of NEAT.

_____   swinging your feet while sitting

_____   reading a book

_____   tapping a pencil on a table

_____   folding laundry

_____   talking on the phone

_____   watching TV

_____   playing a video game

✓ Think About It

1. List the labor-saving devices you used today.

_____

_____

_____

2. Which of these devices was available 50 years ago?

_____

_____

_____

✓ Apply It

*Keep track of where you eat each meal for a week. Use **H** for home, **S** for someone else's home, and **O** for out in a restaurant.*

Day	Breakfast	Lunch	Dinner	Snacks
Sunday				
Monday				
Tuesday				
Wednesday				
Thursday				
Friday				
Saturday				

Total **H:** _____   Total **S:** _____   Total **O:** _____

What did you learn about your dining habits?

_____

_____

_____

✓ Test It

1. The hormone produced in fat tissue that helps regulate body fat is

    a. ghrelin.

    b. leptin.

    c. cholecystokinin.

    d. satiety.

2. One reason Americans are getting larger is that _____ than in past decades.

    a. more time is spent in food preparation

    b. more people work at home

    c. they have fewer children

    d. they spend more time working

How Can You Lose Weight Healthfully?

✔ Know It

Check any of the strategies below that would be healthful for weight loss.

_____ eat more fruits and vegetables

_____ cut back on complex carbohydrates

_____ avoid all fat

_____ eat multiple small meals during the day

_____ include guar gum or chitosan in your diet

_____ eat a moderate amount of protein

_____ cut back on full-fat dairy products

_____ walk for 30 minutes daily

✔ Find It

Check any of the following that are false statements that hype fad diets.

_____ Eat as much meat as you can stuff in.

_____ Don't eat anything white.

_____ The exact combination of foods is important.

_____ Only eat fruits in the morning.

_____ Use low-fat dairy products.

_____ Lose up to seven pounds in a week.

_____ You must use this newly discovered formula along with a diet.

✔ Think About It

Suggest alternative items to lower the calories in the following meals.

Ham and Cheese Omelet	Cheeseburger	Fried Chicken
Fried Potatoes	on a Bun	Cheese Mashed Potatoes
Pancakes with	French Fries	Buttered Corn
Syrup and Butter	Chocolate Shake	Caesar Salad

_____ _____ _____

_____ _____ _____

_____ _____ _____

_____ _____ _____

✔ Apply It

Keep a food log for a day. Note the meal, time eaten, food eaten, and where you ate, and rank your hunger level 1 to 5 (1 = not hungry, 5 = very hungry).

Meal	Time Eaten	What I Ate	Where I Ate It	Hunger Level

Did you eat when you weren't hungry? If so, why?

_____

_____

_____

✔ Test It

1. To lose weight healthfully
    a. cut out at least one meal a day.
    b. eat a high-protein diet.
    c. focus on nutrient-dense foods.
    d. avoid animal products.

2. Behavior modification techniques include
    a. keeping a food log, controlling environmental cues, and managing stress.
    b. eating while doing homework, and avoiding eating fruit and meat together.
    c. eating only when standing up, limiting fluid intake, and not eating after 6 p.m.
    d. eating with others, exercising before bed, and eating crunchy vegetables when stressed.

How Can You Maintain Weight Loss?

✔ Know It

Check the habits that have successfully helped individuals to maintain weight loss.

_____ skip breakfast daily

_____ eat small frequent meals

_____ maintain a high level of physical activity

_____ check weight twice a day

_____ monitor calorie intake

_____ have a positive attitude

✔ Find It

Circle the phrase describing a positive behavior change strategy for weight maintenance.

1. breakfast at home *or* breakfast on the way to work

2. coffee break in the break room *or* walking around the building during breaks

3. walking on a treadmill *or* sitting in a sauna

4. going out for lunch *or* bringing a lunch from home

5. meeting for dinner and a movie *or* meeting for a hike and a picnic

✔ Think About It

Your aunt is an expert on weight loss. She has tried multiple programs and gadgets. Although initially she loses weight, each time she seems to gain the weight back plus a few extra pounds.

1. What is your aunt experiencing?

_____

_____

2. If you could offer her some advice, what would it be?

_____

_____

✔ Apply It

Individuals who lose weight are advised to engage in 60 to 90 minutes of moderate physical activity daily. Outline your plans for physical activity for the next five days.

Day	Plan for Activity	Amount Accomplished

1. Were you able to carry out your plan for physical activity? Why or why not?

_____

_____

_____

2. Could you carry through on this plan next week?

_____

✔ Test It

1. Weight cycling can lead to
   a. hypotension.
   b. elevated HDL cholesterol.
   c. depression and frustration.
   d. cancer.

2. After people lose weight, they
   a. have lower overall energy needs.
   b. can eat more calories to maintain weight loss.
   c. should avoid muscle-building activities.
   d. should not eat before 6 a.m. or after 6 p.m.

How Can You Gain Weight Healthfully?

✔ Know It

Check all of the following that are healthful techniques for weight gain.

_____   eat nutrient-dense foods

_____   avoid physical activity

_____   eat more often during the day

_____ drink beverages with calories

_____ fry all foods

_____ enjoy candy throughout the day

✔ Find It

Circle the food choice that would help an underweight person gain weight.

1. Cheerios *or* granola

2. applesauce *or* apple

3. low-fat milk *or* chocolate low-fat milk *or* whole milk

4. plain low-fat yogurt *or* fruit flavored low-fat yogurt

5. chicken salad *or* chicken breast

6. baked potato *or* mashed potato

✔ Think About It

A friend of yours is constantly teased about her weight and jokingly called " Skinny Mini." Although she feebly protests the teasing and names, most of your friends think she doesn't have anything to worry about. What do you think?

_____

_____

_____

✔ Apply It

List healthy snacks you would be willing to carry as calorie boosters.

_____

_____

_____

✓ Test It

1. Someone trying to gain weight should
    a. load up on high-fat foods.
    b. add sugar to foods.
    c. eat nutrient-dense foods.
    d. eat out more often.

2. To add about a pound of weight weekly,
    a. eat at least 500 calories extra a day.
    b. eat at least 1,000 calories extra a day.
    c. subtract 250 calories of physical activity.
    d. eat at least 3,500 calories extra a day.

Extreme Measures for Extreme Obesity

✓ Know It

Match each term to the appropriate description.

_____ 1. BMI greater than 40

_____ 2. diet of less than 800 calories per day

_____ 3. surgical procedure to reduce size of stomach using staples

_____ 4. surgical procedure to reduce size of stomach using a silicon band

_____ 5. surgical removal of subcutaneous fat

_____ 6. drug that reduces hunger and increases thermogenesis

_____ 7. drug that prevents fat breakdown and absorption

a. orlistat (Xenical)

b. gastric banding

c. sibutramine (Meridia)

d. very low-calorie diet

e. extreme obesity

f. liposuction

g. gastric bypass

✔ Find It

Identify side effects of obesity treatments (each may apply to more than one).

_____	1. very low-calorie diets	a.	electrolyte imbalance
_____	2. gastric bypass surgery	b.	fatigue
_____	3. gastric banding	c.	B_{12} deficiency
_____	4. liposuction	d.	gallstones
_____	5. orlistat (Xenical)	e.	bleeding
		f.	frequent stools, flatulence

✔ Think About It

A classmate is hoping to qualify for gastric banding surgery. He believes this will be the answer to his weight issues. At his first screening appointment, the surgeon said he didn't weigh enough to have the surgery. He is contemplating visiting another center. What advice should your classmate receive?

_____

_____

_____

✔ Apply It

1. Look through your local daily newspaper. How many advertisements are there for centers that specialize in

   gastric bypass surgery? _____

   gastric banding? _____

   liposuction? _____

   weight-loss medications? _____

2. What can you summarize about the marketing of these procedures and products?

_____

_____

_____

✔ Test It

1. _____ is a cosmetic surgical procedure.
   a. Gastric bypass
   b. Gastric banding
   c. Orlistat
   d. Liposuction

2. Prescription weight-loss medications
   a. can replace low-calorie diets.
   b. mean that strenuous exercise is not needed for weight loss.
   c. should be used together with diet and exercise.
   d. make behavior change easier.

What Is Disordered Eating and How Can You Identify It?

✔ Know It

Match the eating disorder to a diagnostic criterion. (Each disorder may be applied to more than one diagnostic criterion.)

_____	1. weight less than 85 percent of expected weight	a. anorexia nervosa
_____	2. recurrent episodes of binge eating	b. bulimia nervosa
_____	3. fear of gaining weight	c. eating disorder not otherwise specified
_____	4. recurrent purging	

_____ 5. overconcern with body shape and weight

_____ 6. binging without purging

_____ 7. consuming most calories during the night

_____ 8. absence of menstrual cycles

✔ Find It

Check any of the following that are examples of purging behavior.

_____ vomiting after eating

_____ excessive exercise

_____ use of laxatives

_____ eating a large amount in a short time

_____ fasting

_____ eating during the night

✔ Think About It

One of your roommates never eats with the rest of you. She claims she has already eaten or is not hungry. You find food wrappers stuffed in her closet. She has become moody and accused you of spying on her.

1. What do you suspect?

_____

_____

2. What will you do?

_____

_____

✔ Apply It

Complete this self-assessment. Are you displaying at-risk eating behavior?

Are You at Risk for an Eating Disorder?

Check the appropriate box in the following statements to help you find out.

1. I constantly think about eating, weight, and body size.   Yes ☐   No ☐
2. I'm terrified about being overweight.   Yes ☐   No ☐
3. I binge eat and can't stop until I feel sick.   Yes ☐   No ☐
4. I weigh myself several times each day.   Yes ☐   No ☐
5. I exercise too much or get very rigid about my exercise plan.   Yes ☐   No ☐
6. I have taken laxatives or forced myself to vomit after eating.   Yes ☐   No ☐
7. I believe food controls my life.   Yes ☐   No ☐
8. I feel extremely guilty after eating.   Yes ☐   No ☐
9. I eat when I am nervous, anxious, lonely, or depressed.   Yes ☐   No ☐
10. I believe my weight controls what I do.   Yes ☐   No ☐

Answer

These statements are designed to help you identify potentially problematic eating behavior. These statements do *not* tell you if you have an eating disorder. Look carefully at any statement you marked as yes and decide if this behavior prevents you from enjoying life or makes you unhealthy. Changing these behaviors should be done gradually, making small changes one at a time. Contact your student health services center or your health care provider if you suspect you need help.

✔ Test It

1.   Anorexia nervosa is characterized by

     a.   recurrent purging to prevent weight gain.

     b.   binge eating at least twice a week.

     c.   eating at night.

     d.   self-starvation.

2.   Binging without purge behavior is classified as

     a.   bulimia nervosa.

     b.   anorexia nervosa.

     c.   eating disorder not otherwise specified.

     d.   obesity.

How Are Disordered Eating Behaviors Treated?

✔ Know It

Match the therapy to the appropriate health care professional. (Each health care professional may be matched to more than one therapy.)

_____ 1. monitors physical symptoms

_____ 2. deals with emotional issues

_____ 3. prescribes medication

_____ 4. establishes normal eating behaviors

_____ 5. makes the diagnosis of an eating disorder

_____ 6. develops meal plans

a. physician

b. psychologist/counselor

c. dietitian

✔ Find It

Check nutritional approaches to treating an eating disorder.

_____ developing a meal plan

_____ identifying foods that trigger a binge

_____ finding appropriate clothes to wear

_____ determining when you are hungry

_____ food and mood journaling

_____ hair analysis

✔ Think About It

A friend admitted that she was struggling with disordered eating behavior. Her mother took her to their small-town family physician. The physician sternly lectured her on the dangers of eating disorders and ordered her to grow up and stop what she was doing. What kind of help does your friend need?

_____

_____

_____

✔ Apply It

1. What services does your campus have available for students struggling with an eating disorder?

    _____

    _____

    _____

2. Does your school have professionals with expertise in the treatment of eating disorders? _____

3. Is medical help available? _____

4. Is counseling available? _____

5. Is nutritional therapy available? _____

6. How long does it take to get an appointment? _____

✔ Test It

1. A dietitian can
    a. diagnose an eating disorder.
    b. prescribe medication or herbal supplements.
    c. help to establish a normal eating plan.
    d. help deal with emotional stress.

2. The best treatment for disordered eating behavior is

   a. time.

   b. a multidisciplinary approach.

   c. a strict meal plan.

   d. inpatient medical treatment.

Two Points of View

Weighing the Pros and Cons of Gastric Bypass Surgery

Read two professionals' opinions on this topic at the end of the chapter in your textbook, then consider the following questions:

1. What criteria must be met before an adolescent can be considered for gastric bypass surgery?

   _____

   _____

   _____

2. According to the experts, what are the benefits of this surgery?

   _____

   _____

   _____

3. What are the risks?

   _____

   _____

   _____

4. In your opinion, do the benefits outweigh the risks?

_____

_____

_____

5. According to Shelley Kirk, adolescents being considered for bariatric surgery should have failed six months of attempts at weight loss. Do you think this is long enough? Why or why not?

_____

_____

_____

6. Dr. Kirk then says the client must be capable of and willing to adhere to nutritional guidelines after surgery. Do these statements sound contradictory?

_____

_____

_____

7. What is the success rate of this surgery?

_____

_____

_____

8. Do you think this is an acceptable success rate?

_____

_____

_____

9. What other surgeries may someone expect as a result of bariatric surgery?

_____

_____

_____

10. What else would you want to know about gastric bypass surgery?

_____

_____

_____

11. Do you think you could follow the postsurgical diet for life?

_____

_____

_____

12. What is your opinion of this surgery for middle-aged people, adolescents, and children?

_____

_____

_____

11 Nutrition and Fitness

What Is Fitness and Why Is It Important?

✓ Know It

Match each term to the appropriate description.

_____ 1. acquired through physical activity and adequate nutrition

_____ 2. voluntary movement that burns calories

_____ 3. structured physical activity

_____ 4. ability to sustain prolonged exercise

_____ 5. amount of force exerted by the muscle

_____ 6. ability of the muscle to produce prolonged effect

_____ 7. exercising with weights

a. muscle strength

b. muscle endurance

c. exercise

d. body composition

e. physical fitness

f. flexibility

g. cardiorespiratory endurance

_____ 8. range of motion   h. physical activity

_____ 9. proportion of fat and lean body tissues   i. weight training

✔ Find It

Check all of the following that are benefits of physical fitness.

_____ insomnia

_____ increased HDL cholesterol

_____ higher blood pressure

_____ less visceral fat

_____ increased insulin sensitivity

_____ reduced risk of osteoporosis

_____ improved hair growth

_____ enhanced immune system

✔ Think About It

A new fitness center is advertising "exercise without effort." All you need to do is position yourself on various pieces of equipment, relax, and let the machines move parts of your body.

1. Does this sound like a total fitness program?

   _____

2. What component of fitness might be met here?

   _____

3. Which components are lacking?

   _____

✔ Apply It

Wear a pedometer for a day. Keep track of your

1. Total number of steps _____

2. Steps getting around school _____

3. Steps getting to and from school and/or work _____

4. Steps at home _____

5. Summarize your activities of daily living.

_____

_____

_____

✔ Test It

1. The greatest amount of force exerted by the muscles at one time is
   a. muscle strength.
   b. muscle endurance.
   c. weight training.
   d. flexibility.

2. The ability to run or bike for a long time is a function of
   a. physical activity.
   b. muscle endurance.
   c. muscle strength.
   d. cardiorespiratory endurance.

What Does a Fitness Program Look Like?

✓ Know It

Unscramble the letters to find the terms defined.

with oxygen   CEBOARI

    — — — — — — —

amount of blood pumped
with each heart beat   RKETSO UOLVEM

    — — — — — —   — — — — — —

level of difficulty   NNITTIYES

    — — — — — — — —

length of time   TONDARUI

    — — — — — — — —

how often you do an activity   RUEQNEYCF

    — — — — — — — — —

✓ Find It

*Determine the fitness area each of the following activities benefits. Use a **C** for cardiorespiratory fitness, **M** for muscular strength, and **F** for flexibility.*

_____ weight lifting

_____ jogging three miles

_____ moving furniture

_____ paddling a kayak

_____ Pilates

_____ ballet

_____ step aerobics class

✔ Think About It

Your friend decides to start an exercise program. He stretches, then takes off running at a quick pace. He lasts 8 minutes at this pace before collapsing in the grass.

1. What was your friend's Rating of Perceived Exertion? _____

2. What advice do you have for him as he starts his exercise program?

    _____

    _____

    _____

✔ Apply It

Chart your activity for three days. Check the areas of fitness that you include and your Rating of Perceived Exertion (RPE).

Day	Activity	Aerobic	Strength	Flexibility	RPE

1. What areas of fitness do you need to change?

    _____

    _____

2. What do you plan to do?

    _____

    _____

✔ Test It

1. Sedentary activities include

   a. doing the dishes and vacuuming the floor.

   b. strolling through the park and shooting baskets.

   c. sitting in class and playing computer games.

   d. a Pilates class.

2. An RPE of 8 to 9 equates to

   a. no noticeable effect.

   b. a slight sweat on a warm day.

   c. somewhat hard.

   d. being able to talk during exercise.

How Are Carbohydrate, Fat, and Protein Used during Exercise?

✔ Know It

Complete the crossword puzzle.

Across

1 maximizing glycogen stores
4 broken down to produce energy
6 with oxygen
8 primary energy source for high-intensity activity
9 primary storage site of glycogen

Down

2 without oxygen
3 acid by-product of rapid glucose metabolism
5 builds and repairs muscle
7 energy source for low-intensity activity

✓ Find It

Match each nutrient type to the activity that uses it. Use **C** *for carbohydrate,* **P** *for protein, and* **F** *for fat.*

_____ running up five flights of stairs

_____ biking for 10 miles

_____ folding laundry

_____ recovering from a marathon

_____ low-level aerobics

_____ chopping wood

✓ Think About It

The equipment at the fitness center can monitor your heart rate and tell when you are in the "fat-burning zone." You notice you need to work harder on some pieces of equipment to be in the zone. Should you avoid that equipment? Why or why not?

_____

_____

✓ Apply It

1. Write a preexercise meal for yourself (1 to 4.5 grams of carbohydrate per kilogram of body weight).

    _____

    _____

2. Write a plan for postexercise nourishment.

    _____

    _____

✔ Test It

1. The primary energy source at the beginning of a five-mile run is

    a. muscle glycogen.

    b. blood glycogen.

    c. adipose tissue.

    d. amino acids.

2. After exercising for over 2 hours, intensity _____ and _____ becomes the primary energy source.

    a. increases; carbohydrate

    b. decreases; carbohydrate

    c. decreases; fat

    d. plateaus; protein

What Vitamins and Minerals Are Important for Fitness?

✔ Know It

Match each nutrient to the appropriate description.

_____ 1. antioxidants   a. vitamins E and C

_____ 2. structural component of hemoglobin   b. anemia

_____ 3. low level of iron in the blood   c. calcium

_____ 4. breaking down of red blood cells   d. iron

_____ 5. maintains bone health   e. hemolysis

✔ Find It

Check the conditions below that are improved with good nutrition.

_____   muscle strain or sprain

_____   iron-deficiency anemia

_____   intravascular hemolysis

_____   sports anemia

_____   blood clotting

_____   muscle contraction

_____   bone loss

✔ Think About It

A classmate has been diagnosed with iron-deficiency anemia. How can this be treated?

_____

_____

✔ Apply It

Survey a group of athletes. Determine the nutrient supplements each commonly uses.

Name	Gender	Supplements Used

1. How many athletes did not use any supplements? _____

2. How many athletes used at least one supplement? _____

3. Do you think their use of a supplement was justified? Why or why not?

_____

_____

_____

_____

_____

✔ Test It

1. Antioxidant nutrients include
    a. carbohydrate.
    b. calcium.
    c. vitamins E and C.
    d. iron.

2. Iron-deficiency anemia
    a. is a greater risk for men.
    b. results from intravascular hemolysis.
    c. is seldom seen in active people.
    d. can be a result of poor eating habits.

How Does Fluid Intake Affect Fitness?

✓ Know It

Match each term to the appropriate description.

_____ 1. loss of body water

_____ 2. primary electrolytes in sweat

_____ 3. dehydration after a short time

_____ 4. dehydration over a long time

_____ 5. low levels of blood sodium

a. acute

b. hyponatremia

c. chronic

d. dehydration

e. sodium and chloride

✓ Find It

Check the best fluids to drink prior to exercise.

_____ water

_____ Gatorade

_____ creme soda

_____ apple juice

_____ Slimfast

_____ coffee

_____ beer

✓ Think About It

After training for a number of days in hot, humid weather, most of the soccer team seems lethargic. What suggestions could you give to the coach?

_____

_____

_____

✓ Apply It

Calculating Your Fluid Needs for Endurance Exercise

The next time you take a 1-hour training run, use the following process to determine your fluid needs.

1. Make sure that you are properly hydrated before the workout. Your urine should be clear.
2. Do a warm-up run to the point where you start to sweat, then stop. Urinate if necessary.
3. Weigh yourself on an accurate scale.
4. Run for one hour at an intensity similar to your targeted race.
5. Drink a measured amount of a beverage of your choice during the run to quench your thirst. Be sure to keep track of how much you drink.
6. Do not urinate during the run.
7. After you have finished the run, weigh yourself again on the same scale you used in step 3.
8. Calculate your fluid needs using the following formula:
   a. Enter your body weight from step 3 in pounds _____
   b. Enter your body weight from step 7 in pounds − _____
   c. Subtract b from a = _____
   × 15.3
   d. Convert the pounds of weight in c to fluid ounces by multiplying by 15.3 _____
   e. Enter the amount of fluid you consumed during the run in ounces + _____
   f. Add e to d = _____

The final figure is the number of ounces of fluid that you must consume per hour to remain well hydrated.

Source: Adapted from D. Casa. _USA Track & Field Self-Testing Program for Optimal Hydration for Distance Running._ Available at www.usatf.org/groups/coaches/library/hydration/ USATFselfTestingProgramForOptimalHydration.pdf

✔ Test It

1. Sports drinks used prior to exercise should contain

   a. carbohydrate, protein, and sodium.

   b. calcium, iron, and electrolytes.

   c. fluid, electrolytes, and carbohydrate.

   d. fluid, sodium, and amino acids.

2. The American College of Sports Medicine recommends _____ 2 to 3 hours before exercise.

   a. abstaining from solid food

   b. drinking one cup of fluid per kilogram of body weight

   c. taking glucose or maltodextrin

   d. drinking two to three cups of fluid

Can Dietary Supplements Contribute to Fitness?

✔ Know It

First, fill in the letters for the terms described. Then transfer the numbered letters to complete the heading of the terms.

__ __ __ __ __ __ __ __ __   __ __ __
3 2 9 7 9 3 6 5 1   4 5 8

__ __ __ __ T __ __ __   may increase ATP generated
1 2 3 4   5 6 3

__ __ F F __ __ __ __   may increase availability of fatty acids
1 4   3 5 6 3   during exercise

__ __ __ B __ L __ __   S T __ __ __ __ __   testosterone-based substance
4 6 4   7   5 1   3 2 7 5 8

__ __ __ W T H   H __ __ M __ __ __   produced in the pituitary gland
9 2 7   7 2   7 6 3

__ __ Y T H __ __ P __ __ __ T __ __   hormone produced by the kidneys
3 2   2 7 7 5 3   5 6

B L __ __ __   __ __ P __ __ __   red blood cell infusion
    7 7 8   8 7   5 6 9

✔ Find It

Match the ergogenic aids to their possible side effects.

_____ 1. increase blood viscosity

_____ 2. reduce body fat in trained athletes

_____ 3. androgenic effects

_____ 4. death

_____ 5. acromegaly

_____ 6. dehydration

_____ 7. tumor development

a. caffeine

b. anabolic steroids

c. growth hormone

d. erythropoietin

✔ Think About It

It sounds too good to be true! A simple daily injection can reduce body fat and increase fat-free tissue. The product is the same hormone produced by the body: growth hormone. What harm could come from giving this a try?

_____

_____

✔ Apply It

Go to the NCAA website. Which of the supplements listed below are banned for use by NCAA intercollegiate athletes?

Supplement	Banned? Yes or No
creatine	
caffeine	
epinephrine	
anabolic steroids	
growth hormone	
erythropoietin	
amino acids	

✓ Test It

1. Supplements targeted toward athletes

   a. have proven effective.

   b. have definite ergogenic effects.

   c. are inexpensive.

   d. are not strictly regulated by the Food and Drug Administration.

2. Creatine may have a benefit in

   a. sprint running.

   b. weight lifting.

   c. marathon skiing.

   d. weight loss.

Two Points of View

Are Personal Trainers Reliable Sources of Credible Nutrition Information?

Read two professionals' opinions on this topic at the end of the chapter in your textbook, then consider the following questions:

1. How does someone become a qualified personal trainer?

   _____

   _____

2. Do you think this training is rigorous?

   _____

   _____

3. Does certification as a trainer mean the person is an expert in fitness planning for healthy people?

   _____

   _____

4. Does certification as a trainer mean the person is an expert in activity planning for someone with chronic disease?

_____

_____

5. According to Brenda Malinauskas, only Registered Dietitians are qualified to give nutrition information. Do you agree? Why or why not?

_____

_____

6. If you have nutrition questions, to whom would you turn? Why?

_____

_____

12

Lifecycle Nutrition
Pregnancy through Infancy

How Does a Baby Begin Developing?

✓ Know It

Match each term to the appropriate description.

_____	1.	three time periods of pregnancy	a.	placenta
_____	2.	a sperm fertilizes an egg	b.	fetus
_____	3.	first two weeks after conception	c.	conception
_____	4.	three- to eight-week-old fertilized egg	d.	umbilical cord
_____	5.	exchange site between mother and embryo	e.	embryo
_____	6.	attaches placenta to fetus	f.	trimesters
_____	7.	eight-week-old developing embryo	g.	zygote

✔ Find It

Number the stages of development in order from 1 to 5.

_____   embryo

_____   fetus

_____   conception

_____   preembryo

_____   zygote

✔ Think About It

Knowing that the placenta exchanges nutrients, oxygen, and waste products between the mother and the developing fetus, what environments should the mother avoid?

_____

_____

_____

✔ Apply It

If you could chart your future, at what age would you choose to become a parent? Why?

_____

_____

_____

✔ Test It

1. _____ refers to a fertilized egg for the first two weeks after conception.

   a. Implantation

   b. Embryo

   c. Preembryo

   d. Zygote

2. The moment when a sperm fertilizes an egg is

   a. conception.

   b. implantation.

   c. embryo.

   d. placenta.

What Nutrients and Behaviors Are Most Important for a Healthy Pregnancy?

✔ Know It

Use a plus (+) sign to indicate behaviors fathers- and mothers-to-be should adopt. Use a negative (−) sign to indicate behaviors to avoid.

_____ smoking

_____ eating a variety of fruits and vegetables

_____ snacking on nuts

_____ ingesting botanicals

_____ drinking a few cups of coffee

_____ eating tuna for lunch daily

_____ drinking a couple of glasses of wine with dinner

_____ socializing in a smoke-filled bar

_____ eating lean meat products

✔ Find It

Match the nutrient, chemical, or behavior with possible effects on pregnancy.

_____ 1. neural tube defects

_____ 2. hypertension

_____ 3. low birth weight

_____ 4. nervous system

_____ 5. risk of miscarriage

_____ 6. sudden infant death syndrome

_____ 7. reduced fertility

a. underweight

b. methylmercury in fish

c. caffeine

d. folic acid

e. cigarette smoking

f. obesity

g. marijuana

✔ Think About It

Your older sister works two jobs, the evening one as a cocktail waitress. She and her partner eat out for most meals and enjoy the party scene. She says that she would like to have a baby within the next year. What healthy behaviors will she need to adopt to increase the likelihood of a healthy outcome?

_____

_____

_____

✔ Apply It

Are You Nutritionally Ready for a Healthy Pregnancy?

Both males and females should have healthy habits before becoming parents. Take the following self-assessment to see if you need some diet and lifestyle fine tuning before trying to get pregnant.

For Both Men and Women

1. Are you overweight?
   Yes ☐ **No** ☐
2. Do you smoke?
   Yes ☐ **No** ☐
3. Do you abuse alcohol?
   Yes ☐ **No** ☐
4. Do you consume less than 400 micrograms of folic acid daily?
   Yes ☐ **No** ☐
5. Do you use any illicit drugs such as marijuana, cocaine, and/or Ecstasy?
   Yes ☐ **No** ☐

Additional Questions for Women Only

1. Do you drink alcohol?
   Yes ☐ **No** ☐
2. Do you take herbs or use herbal teas?
   Yes ☐ **No** ☐
3. Do you drink more than 12 ounces of caffeinated coffee or energy drinks or four cans of caffeinated soft drinks daily?
   Yes ☐ **No** ☐
4. Do you eat albacore tuna, swordfish, mackerel, tilefish, and/or shark?
   Yes ☐ **No** ☐

If you answered "yes" to any of the questions, what can you do to increase your chances of a healthy pregnancy?

_____

_____

✔ Test It

1. A low birth weight baby

    a. is likely to become an obese child.

    b. weighs less than 5½ pounds at birth.

    c. will often have a neural tube defect.

    d. is desirable for ease of delivery.

2. Sudden infant death syndrome (SIDS) is related to

    a. methylmercury in fish.

    b. caffeine in coffee.

    c. exposure to cigarette smoke.

    d. maternal obesity.

In the First Trimester

✔ Know It

Match each term to the appropriate description.

_____	1. excessive vomiting during pregnancy	a.	raw meat and fish
_____	2. heightens perception of odors	b.	estrogen
_____	3. eating nonfood substances	c.	iron
_____	4. prenatal supplement needed	d.	hyperemesis gravidarum
_____	5. increased risk of birth defects	e.	sugar substitutes
_____	6. FDA deemed acceptable	f.	vitamin A
_____	7. cause of foodborne illnesses	g.	pica

✔ Find It

Check the possible treatments for morning sickness.

_____   wait until afternoon for symptoms to leave

_____   small, frequent meals

_____   aspirin or ibuprofen

_____   carbohydrates such as rice, pasta, and crackers

_____   vitamin B_6

_____   potato chips and lemonade

_____   ginger ale

_____   fruits and vegetables

_____   chili powder

✔ Think About It

A classmate is suffering with the early effects of pregnancy, including morning sickness. She generally skips breakfast and sips on broth for lunch. What are recommendations for your classmate?

_____

_____

_____

_____

✔ Apply It

Complete the chart below.

Components of Healthy Weight Gain during Pregnancy

Component	Pounds
maternal fat	7
	4
blood	
	7
placenta and other fluids	
TOTAL	25–35

✔ Test It

1. Hyperemesis gravidarum is

    a. common in most pregnant women.

    b. due to a deficiency of estrogen.

    c. a serious complication needing medical treatment.

    d. caused by eating spicy or greasy foods.

2. The recommended weight gain during pregnancy for an average woman is

    a. 34 to 40 pounds.

    b. 25 to 35 pounds.

    c. 15 to 20 pounds.

    d. 12 to 15 pounds.

In the Second Trimester

✔ Know It

Match each term to the appropriate description.

_____ 1. diabetes that occurs during pregnancy

_____ 2. large baby

_____ 3. yellowish coloring of skin due to bile pigments

_____ 4. hypertension and edema

_____ 5. low blood glucose

a. preeclampsia

b. gestational diabetes

c. hypoglycemia

d. jaundice

e. macrosomia

✔ Find It

Check the risk factors for gestational diabetes.

_____ obesity

_____ underweight

_____ over 25 years old

_____ 16 to 18 years old

_____ history of high glucose levels

_____ African American or Native American

_____ previously given birth to a very large baby

✔ Think About It

A friend becomes pregnant and is determined to maintain her fitness regime. She is an avid downhill skier, lifts weights, and practices yoga. What exercise recommendations should be given to this mother-to-be?

_____

_____

_____

✔ Apply It

Write a menu to meet the nutritional needs of a normal healthy woman in her second trimester of pregnancy.

Breakfast	Lunch	Dinner	Snacks

✔ Test It

1. Gestational diabetes is more common in
    a. teenage mothers.
    b. women of European descent.
    c. Native American woman.
    d. women with hypoglycemia.

2. The cure for preeclampsia is
    a. a low-sodium diet.
    b. antihypertensive medications.
    c. delivery of the baby.
    d. moderate exercise.

In the Third Trimester

✔ Know It

Check the common physical complaints that occur during the third trimester of pregnancy.

_____   hair loss

_____   difficulty climbing stairs

_____   problems sleeping

_____   morning sickness

_____   constipation

_____   heartburn

_____   low back pain

_____   chest pain

✔ Find It

*Use an **H** for techniques that can help alleviate heartburn. Use a **C** if the technique could help alleviate constipation.*

_____ whole grains

_____ fruits and vegetables

_____ small, frequent meals

_____ avoid spicy or highly seasoned food

_____ plenty of fluid

_____ beans and nuts

✔ Think About It

Your pregnant sister-in-law seems to spend all day lying on the couch. She complains of chronic heartburn. What can she do to feel better?

_____

_____

_____

✔ Apply It

Write a meal plan for the extra 450 calories a pregnant woman needs during the third trimester.

Breakfast	Lunch	Dinner	Snacks

Test It

1. Constipation may be helped with

    a. addition of iron in prenatal supplements.

    b. limitation of fluid intake.

    c. avoidance of physical activity.

    d. plenty of fresh fruits and vegetables.

2. Heartburn is

    a. a serious medical condition.

    b. the reflux of stomach contents into the esophagus.

    c. a warning of impending heart attack.

    d. caused by anemia.

What Special Concerns Might Younger or Older Mothers-to-Be Face?

✓ Know It

*Use a **T** if the concern is for a pregnant teen. Use an **O** if the concern applies more to a mother over age 35.*

_____   high nutrient needs for growth

_____   pregnancy-induced hypertension

_____   gestational diabetes

_____   low birth weight baby

_____   problems conceiving

_____   likely to engage in unhealthy lifestyle habits

✔ Find It

Check the diet changes teen or older mothers-to-be should adopt.

_____   get adequate folic acid

_____   avoid caffeine

_____   chew sugar-free gum

_____   avoid alcohol

_____   eat fruits and vegetables

_____   drink diet soda

_____   include low-fat dairy products

✔ Think About It

The public secondary school in your community sponsors a program for pregnant teens and you're helping to write a pamphlet to distribute regarding proper nutrition. What nutritional concerns should be addressed in the pamphlet?

_____

_____

_____

_____

✔ Apply It

Interview a pregnant woman.

1. What are her particular nutritional concerns?

_____

_____

2. Did or does she experience morning sickness? If so, how did or does she treat it? _____

_____

3. Is she taking a prenatal vitamin? _____

4. What particular foods does she avoid?

_____

_____

5. Has she noted any food cravings?

_____

_____

✔ Test It

1. Fertility typically declines in
   a. teens aged 14 to 16.
   b. women aged 20 to 30.
   c. women over age 30.
   d. women over age 50.

2. _____ should limit caffeine intake and avoid alcohol.
   a. Pregnant teens
   b. Pregnant women over age 30
   c. All pregnant women
   d. Dads-to-be

What Is Breast-Feeding and Why Is It Beneficial?

✓ Know It

Match each term to the appropriate description.

_____	1. feeding an infant from a woman's breast	a.	oxytocin
_____	2. production of milk after childbirth	b.	breast-feeding
_____	3. release of milk from the mother's breast	c.	colostrum
_____	4. hormone that causes milk to be produced	d.	prolactin
_____	5. hormone that causes milk to be released	e.	lactation
_____	6. first fluid expressed from the breast after childbirth	f.	let-down

✓ Find It

Check the items below that are benefits of breast-feeding for an infant.

_____ reduces blood loss

_____ promotes bonding with the mother

_____ reduces risk of chronic diseases

_____ provides immune protection

_____ helps intellectual development

_____ increases risk of obesity

✔ Find It, Too

Check the items below that are benefits of breast-feeding for a mother.

_____ quicker return to prepregnancy size and shape

_____ reduces risk of breast cancer

_____ promotes bonding with the infant

_____ can be considered a disability excusable from work

_____ reduces risk of chronic disease

_____ helps increase intellectual intelligence

_____ saves money

✔ Think About It

A pregnant friend is contemplating breast-feeding her infant. One of her dilemmas is that she will only have two months off of work after delivery. She wonders if it's even worth giving lactation a try for just two months. What do you think?

_____

_____

✔ Apply It

1. What does your work or school environment do to support breast-feeding mothers?

    _____

    _____

2. Is there a place a lactating woman can go to express and store her milk?

    _____

3. Would she have adequate break time to do that?

    _____

4. What accommodations do you think need to be made?

_____

_____

✓ Test It

1. Breast-feeding may help to reduce
   a. risk of childhood obesity.
   b. maternal obesity.
   c. intellectual development.
   d. bonding.

2. The first fluid expressed from the breast after birth is
   a. oxytocin.
   b. prolactin.
   c. colostrum.
   d. insulin.

What Are the Best Dietary and Lifestyle Habits for a Breast-Feeding Mother?

✓ Know It

Circle the best answer.

1. To meet increased fluid needs, a breast-feeding woman should drink (8 *or* 13) cups of beverages daily.

2. She also needs (500 *or* 750) extra calories daily.

3. Some of these calories can come from body (muscle *or* fat) stores.

4. During the second six months of breast-feeding, a lactating woman needs (a greater *or* a lesser *or* about the same) amount of calories as she did during the second and third trimesters of pregnancy.

✔ Find It

Check all of the following that might be passed to an infant through breast milk.

_____ caffeine

_____ sugar substitutes

_____ alcohol

_____ contaminants the mother consumes

_____ nicotine

_____ flavors from spicy foods

_____ fluid

✔ Think About It

A friend is breast-feeding her infant. As she is doing this, she sips on a glass of wine. She says that wine helps her to relax and helps the baby to sleep longer at night. What do you think of this practice?

_____

_____

✔ Apply It

Design a small poster or bumper sticker promoting the benefits of breast-feeding.

✔ Test It

1. During the first six months of breast-feeding, the mother produces about _____ of milk daily.
   a. 3 to 4 cups
   b. ½ gallon
   c. a pint
   d. ¾ quart

2. During lactation, caffeine should be

    a. eliminated from the diet.

    b. limited to 2 to 3 cups daily.

    c. consumed as desired.

    d. consumed only in the morning.

When Is Formula a Healthy Alternative to Breast Milk?

✓ Know It

Check the reasons why some women should not breast-feed.

_____	AIDS	_____	large breasts
_____	teen mother	_____	taking prescription medications
_____	receiving chemotherapy or radiation	_____	infant has galactosemia
_____	older mother	_____	pierced nipple

✓ Find It

Circle the best answer.

1. The best alternative to breast-feeding is to feed an infant (cow's milk *or* soy milk *or* commercial formula).

2. Cow's milk contains too (much *or* little) protein.

3. Cow's milk is too (low *or* high) in fat and too (low *or* high) in sodium and potassium.

4. The iron in cow's milk is (absorbed well *or* poorly absorbed).

✔ Think About It

Your grandmother has a recipe for infant formula that includes sweetened condensed milk, corn syrup, and water. Her physician had given her this recipe when she had her children and she claims that it worked perfectly fine. What do you think of this formula recipe?

_____

_____

✔ Apply It

Compare infant formulas at the grocery store.

Product Name	Source of Protein	Type (Powdered, Concentrate, Ready-to-Use)	Cost per Serving (4 oz)

1. Summarize your findings.

   _____

   _____

2. If you were in the market for an infant formula, which of these products would you select? Why?

   _____

   _____

✔ Test It

1. Cow's milk does not meet the nutritional needs of an infant because it contains

    a. too much protein.

    b. too little protein.

    c. too much fat.

    d. too little sodium and potassium.

2. An infant born with galactosemia

    a. must be treated with immunosuppressive drugs.

    b. cannot be breast-fed.

    c. should be fed cow's milk.

    d. will die in infancy.

What Are the Nutrient Needs of an Infant and Why Are They So High?

✔ Know It

Check the developmental milestones seen during an infant's first year of life.

_____ suckles

_____ able to hold head up

_____ grows hair

_____ able to sit up

_____ able to chew foods

_____ verbalizes with words

_____ feeds self

✔ Find It

Number the food items from 1 to 5 in the order in which they should be introduced into an infant's diet.

_____   mashed or chopped food from the family meal

_____   iron-fortified infant cereal

_____   breast milk or formula

_____   pureed or strained meat or beans

_____   pureed fruits or vegetables

✔ Think About It

1. What do you think of prepared infant foods?

     _____

     _____

2. What are the advantages of prepared infant foods?

     _____

     _____

3. What are the disadvantages of prepared infant foods?

     _____

     _____

✔ Apply It

1. How much did you weigh at birth? _____ at 6 months? _____

   at 1 year? _____

2. Did you triple your birth weight in a year? _____

3. If you can, look at your infant growth chart. What percentile were you generally in for

   height? _____ weight? _____

4. Do you think those percentiles are still true for you as an adult?

   _____

5. Summarize your first year of life.

   _____

   _____

✔ Test It

1. Generally an infant _____ weight in the first year of life.
   a. doubles
   b. triples
   c. quadruples
   d. loses

2. Nutrients that must be added to an infant's diet include
   a. vitamin B_{12}, folate, and fluoride.
   b. vitamin A, vitamin C, and calcium.
   c. vitamin E, potassium, and sodium.
   d. vitamin K, vitamin D, and iron.

When Are Solid Foods Safe?

✓ Know It

Match each food item to the age when it can generally be offered to a normal infant.

_____ 1. breast milk

_____ 2. rice cereal

_____ 3. pureed vegetables

_____ 4. pureed meats or beans

_____ 5. cow's milk

a. 4 to 6 months

b. 6 to 8 months

c. throughout the first year

d. 6 to 9 months

e. after 1 year

✓ Find It

Check the common food allergens from the list below.

_____ eggs

_____ peanut butter

_____ orange juice

_____ rice

_____ chocolate

_____ bananas

_____ strawberries

_____ cow's milk

✓ Think About It

You observe a fussy young child in a restaurant. The parents are offering mashed foods, but the child is refusing to eat. Finally, the mother gives the child a bottle of milk. The child drinks two bottles of milk and appears content. What do you think of this scenario?

_____

_____

✓ Apply It

Compare infant foods at a grocery store.

Food Item	Container Size	Number of Servings per Container	Cost

1. Would you consider these food items a good buy or too expensive? Why?

_____

_____

2. Would you choose to use these products to feed an infant? Why or why not?

_____

_____

✓ Test It

1. Clostridium botulism can be found in
   a. egg whites.
   b. honey.
   c. cow's milk.
   d. peanut butter.

2. The first solid food that should be offered to an infant is
   a. pureed fruits.
   b. barley or oat cereal.
   c. rice cereal.
   d. graham crackers.

A Taste Could Be Dangerous: Food Allergies

✓ Know It

Match each term to the appropriate description.

_____ 1. abnormal reaction by the immune system to a food

_____ 2. proteins causing an adverse reaction by the immune system

_____ 3. connective tissue cells to which antibodies attach

_____ 4. life-threatening reactions, including constriction of airways

_____ 5. adverse reaction to food that does not involve an immune response

_____ 6. first stage of an immune response to a food allergy

_____ 7. second stage of an immune response to a food allergy

a. allergens

b. food allergy

c. intolerance

d. sensitization

e. anaphylactic

f. allergic reaction

g. mast cells

✓ Find It

Check the foods below that may contain common allergens.

_____ store-bought cookies _____ crackers

_____ ice cream _____ seafood salad

_____ fruit juice _____ frozen entrees

_____ frozen dairy treats _____ wild rice

_____ school lunches

✔ Think About It

A friend has a peanut allergy and generally carries an Epi-Pen. He inadvertently eats a piece of cake with peanut butter in the frosting. He immediately appears to be having a reaction. What should you do?

_____

_____

✔ Apply It

1. Look at a restaurant menu. If you had allergies to eggs, milk, and peanuts, which entrees could you safely order?

    _____

    _____

2. How could you be sure these selections would be free of all allergens?

    _____

    _____

✔ Test It

1. Allergens are
    a. carbohydrates.
    b. fats.
    c. proteins.
    d. free radicals.

2. Stage 1 of an immune response to a food allergen includes
    a. first allergen contact.
    b. histamine being released from mast cells.
    c. itching, swelling, and nausea.
    d. an anaphylactic reaction.

Two Points of View

Choosing Among Baby Foods

Read two professionals' opinions on this topic at the end of the chapter in your textbook, then consider the following questions:

1. What is the purpose of baby foods?

   _____

   _____

2. What are the nutrient differences between commercial baby food and homemade baby food?

   _____

3. How much do commercially prepared baby foods cost?

   _____

   _____

4. Does this sound reasonable or expensive?

   _____

   _____

5. What are the standards for commercially prepared baby foods?

   _____

   _____

6. Both experts highlighted in the **Two Points of View** section work or have worked for a baby food manufacturer. Do you think this affects their opinions of commercial versus homemade baby foods? Give an example.

   _____

   _____

13

Lifecycle Nutrition
Toddlers through the Later Years

Young Children's Nutritional Needs and Issues

✓ Know It

Match each term to the appropriate description.

_____ 1. children aged 1 to 3 years old

a. iron deficiency

_____ 2. children aged 3 to 5 years old

b. iron toxicity

_____ 3. most common nutrient deficiency in young children

c. preschooler

_____ 4. leading cause of death in children under age 6

d. food jag

_____ 5. unwillingness to eat familiar foods

e. toddler

_____ 6. when a child continuously eats only one food

f. picky eater

✔ Find It

Check the items that are choking hazards for young children, then circle the food items that should not be offered to children under age 4.

_____   chewing gum

_____   popcorn

_____   hot dog

_____   raw vegetables

_____   oatmeal

_____   rock

_____   coin

_____   ice cream

How could each choking hazard be modified to make it acceptable?

_____

_____

✔ Think About It

You are babysitting a toddler who will only eat Cheerios. Do you think this is worrisome behavior? What might you do to help the child broaden his food choices?

_____

_____

✔ Apply It

Write down your menu for one day.

Breakfast	Lunch	Dinner	Snacks

Modify your menu to fit the needs of a preschooler.

Breakfast	Lunch	Dinner	Snacks

✔ Test It

1. Recommended portion size for young children is
   a. ½ to 1 cup.
   b. one tablespoon per year of age.
   c. an ounce per year of age.
   d. ¼ of an adult portion.

2. It is the parent's responsibility to
   a. watch how much a child eats.
   b. have a child try everything on her plate.
   c. choose where and when food is offered.
   d. encourage children to clean their plates.

School-Aged Children's Nutritional Needs and Issues

✔ Know It

Check the possible causes of childhood obesity.

_____ access to vending machines	_____ school lunch
_____ overweight parents	_____ limited computer time
_____ drinking sports beverages	_____ television viewing
_____ lack of fruits and vegetables	_____ physical education classes
_____ after-school activities	_____ large portion sizes

✔ Find It

Check the nutrients with minimum requirements in USDA school lunches.

calories   calcium   vitamin C

fat   vitamin B$_{12}$ sodium

carbohydrate   folate   potassium

protein   iron

✔ Think About It

You volunteer for the day in a reading program at a nearby elementary school. During this time the students have a snack break. One of the students is celebrating a birthday and brought cupcakes for the class. The student you are working with is given half of a sliced apple and water. He breaks down crying and begins thrashing about, and is sent to the school nurse. The teacher explains that the student is denied sweet snacks because his mother thinks it contributes to ADHD. What do you think of this scenario?

_____

_____

_____

✔ Apply It

1. Summarize physical activities you have done regularly with your family.

    _____

    _____

2. Would you rate these as more or less than what your friends' families did?

    _____

    _____

3. What hindered your family in being physically active together?

_____

_____

4. If or when you start your own family, what will you do differently in regard to physical activity?

_____

✓ Test It

1. Overweight children should
   a. not be allowed to snack between meals.
   b. drink water with meals.
   c. be restricted in activities.
   d. be encouraged to increase physical activity.

2. Parents and caregivers of overweight children should
   a. sign them up for extracurricular activity classes with peers.
   b. put them on a weight-reduction diet.
   c. model good eating and activity patterns.
   d. not allow them to eat school lunch.

Adolescents' Nutritional Needs and Issues

✓ Know It

Circle the best answer of the choices given.

1. (Adolescence *or* Menarche) is the lifecycle stage between ages 9 and 19.

2. Among the physical changes is the first menstrual cycle, or (growth spurt *or* menarche), in girls.

3. Most bone growth occurs in the (peak bone mass *or* epiphyseal plate), the area of tissue near the end of long bones.

4. Adolescents need (calcium *or* iron) for bone growth.

5. Adolescents may be at risk for (obesity *or* disordered eating).

✔ Find It

Check any of the following items that are social and emotional growth issues of adolescence.

_____   desire for independence

_____   defiance of authority

_____   desire for individuality

_____   media influences

_____   peer influences

_____   low self-esteem

_____   disordered eating behaviors

_____   ignorant parents

✔ Think About It

Marathon running events restrict entry to athletes over age 18. Why would adolescents be prohibited from participating?

_____

_____

✔ Apply It

1. Think back to your high school days. Outline your typical daily meal plan.

_____

_____

2. How has your meal plan changed since attending college?

_____

_____

3. What can you do to improve the nutritional quality of your current meal plan?

_____

_____

✓ Test It

1. Among the physical changes of adolescence is
    a. defiance of authority.
    b. the influence of media and peers.
    c. the ability to get a part-time job.
    d. a rapid growth spurt.

2. Good sources of calcium are often replaced with _____ in adolescent diets.
    a. fast-food burgers
    b. sugar-laden soft drinks
    c. french fries or potato chips
    d. water

Older Adults' Nutritional Issues

✓ Know It

Check any of the following that are physical changes of aging.

_____   need more calories

_____   need fewer calories

_____   vitamin A needs increase

_____   fiber needs decrease

_____ ability to make vitamin D from the sun increases

_____ lose ability to absorb vitamin B_{12}

_____ need for calcium increases

✓ Find It

Match the nutrient with possible food choices.

_____ 1. whole-grain products, fruits, and vegetables   a. zinc

_____ 2. carrots, cantaloupe, sweet potato, broccoli   b. beta-carotene

_____ 3. fortified milk, yogurt, cereal   c. vitamin B_{12}

_____ 4. fortified cereals and soy milk   d. vitamin D

_____ 5. lean meat, fish, and poultry, with citrus fruits   e. iron

_____ 6. lean meats, legumes, nuts, fortified cereals   f. fiber

✓ Think About It

An elderly neighbor has difficulty getting around on her own. She limits her fluid intake. Her typical breakfast is toasted white bread, jam, and tea. Her other meal is often soup and crackers. What nutritional problems might you expect to see?

_____

_____

✓ Apply It

1. Write down the cafeteria menu for one day.

_____

_____

2. Modify the menu to meet the needs of a 70-year-old.

_____

_____

3. What major adjustments were needed?

_____

_____

✓ Test It

1. People are living longer now than in the early 1900s, primarily due to
   a. better transportation.
   b. vaccinations to decrease infectious and deadly diseases.
   c. cleaner air and water.
   d. better genes.

2. Because a person's metabolic rate naturally declines with age, older adults need
   a. fewer calories.
   b. to limit physical activity.
   c. more vitamin A in the form of beta-carotene.
   d. more phytochemicals.

What Additional Challenges May Older Adults Face?

✓ Know It

Match each term to the appropriate description.

_____ 1. inflammation in joints that causes pain   a. Alzheimer's disease

_____ 2. a brain disorder that interferes with memory   b. food insecurity

_____ 3. most common form of dementia   c. alcohol abuse

_____ 4. chronic lack of sufficient food

_____ 5. feelings of grief, sadness, and isolation

_____ 6. alcohol use to calm nerves, reduce stress

d. arthritis

e. depression

f. dementia

✔ Find It

Check possible causes of food insecurity for an older adult.

_____ limited finances

_____ lack of transportation

_____ loss of mate

_____ inability to prepare food

_____ Meals-on-Wheels

_____ tooth or gum disease

_____ alcohol abuse

_____ multiple medications

✔ Think About It

1. Why are congregate meals often served at churches, synagogues, and other community sites?

_____

_____

2. What other services for seniors could be offered besides a meal?

_____

_____

✔ Apply It

Volunteer to assist at a congregate meal site or Meals-on-Wheels program. Write a brief summary of your observations.

_____

_____

_____

_____

✔ Test It

1. Physical activity for older adults
   a. should be avoided to save wear on joints.
   b. needs to be strictly monitored to avoid injury.
   c. can include household chores like gardening and raking leaves.
   d. should be primarily non–weight bearing.

2. It is normal for older adults to
   a. take longer to learn new information.
   b. experience dementia.
   c. develop Alzheimer's disease.
   d. become depressed.

Drugs, Food, and Drug-Herb Interactions

✔ Know It

Match each nutrient or herb to its purported use.

_____   1. prevents osteoporosis

_____   2. lowers blood cholesterol levels

a. ginkgo biloba

b. vitamin K

_____ 3. reduces memory loss   c. calcium

_____ 4. reduces depression   d. St. John's wort

_____ 5. helps blood to clot   e. vitamin E

_____ 6. reduces risk of heart disease   f. garlic

✔ Find It

Check the herbs and nutrients commonly found in food.

_____ calcium		_____ black cohosh
_____ Dong Quai root		_____ vitamin E
_____ echinacea		_____ fish oil
_____ garlic		_____ vitamin K
_____ ginseng		_____ St. John's wort
_____ grapefruit juice		_____ niacin

✔ Think About It

Your older neighbor asked you to pick up his prescription at the neighborhood pharmacy. You notice on the label that it is called a monoamine oxidase inhibitor. What precautions should your neighbor take with this drug?

_____

_____

_____

✔ Apply It

1. Write down the information found on a bottle of an herbal supplement sold at a grocery store.

_____

_____

2. Go to the website for the Food and Drug Administration: www.fda.gov. What does the FDA say about this particular product?

_____

_____

✔ Test It

1. The best professional to consult about food, drug, and herbal interactions is a(n)

    a. dietitian.

    b. pharmacist.

    c. physician.

    d. herbologist.

2. Foods can interact with medications by

    a. delaying the absorption of a drug.

    b. increasing the absorption of a drug.

    c. potentiating the effect of a drug.

    d. doing all of the above.

Two Points of View

Are Schools Out to Lunch?

Read two professionals' opinions on this topic at the end of the chapter in your textbook, then consider the following questions:

1. What is a commodity food?

    _____

    _____

2. How do school lunch programs contribute to childhood obesity? Give an example from one of the experts in **Two Points of View.**

    _____

    _____

3. According to Antonia Demas, does school lunch contribute to diseases?

_____

_____

4. According to Antonia Demas, does school lunch contribute to behavior problems in classrooms?

_____

_____

5. Do you agree or disagree with these assessments? Why or why not?

_____

_____

6. How can school lunches be improved?

_____

_____

14

Food Safety and Technology

What Causes Foodborne Illness and How Can It Make You Sick?

✓ Know It

Complete the crossword puzzle.

Across

2   common virus that causes foodborne illness
8   inflammation of stomach and intestine
9   poison

Down

1   common diarrhea caused by unsanitary conditions
3   microscopic living organisms
4   organism that lives on or in another organism
5   microscopic organism that can infect a host
6   disease-causing microbes
7   living plant or animal

✔ Find It

Check the individuals most at risk for foodborne illnesses.

_____   infants

_____   college students

_____   elderly people

_____   someone being treated with chemotherapy or radiation

_____   middle-aged women

_____   someone with AIDS

_____   pregnant women

_____   residents of a group home

✔ Think About It

You are planning a trip to Mexico during spring break. What precautions should you take to avoid traveler's diarrhea?

_____

_____

✔ Apply It

Look through your refrigerator. What foods could be carriers of foodborne illness?

Food Item	Date Purchased or Prepared	Length of Time in Refrigerator

What food items should you get rid of after your inventory?

_____

_____

✔ Test It

1. Viruses must have a living _____, such as a plant or animal, to survive.
    a. pathogen
    b. toxin
    c. bacteria
    d. host

2. Organisms that live on or in another organism are referred to as
    a. hosts.
    b. parasites.
    c. toxins.
    d. pathogens.

What Can You Do to Prevent Foodborne Illness?

✔ Know It

Match each temperature to its specific measurement.

_____	1. room temperature	a.	below 40°F
_____	2. safe zone for hot foods	b.	160°F
_____	3. safe zone for cold foods	c.	0°F
_____	4. danger zone	d.	0°F to 40°F
_____	5. freezer temperature	e.	68°F to 75°F
_____	6. refrigerator temperature	f.	40°F to 140°F
_____	7. well-done beef	g.	≥140°F

✔ Find It

Check possible sources of cross-contamination.

_____ your hands

_____ kitchen counter

_____ kitchen sink

_____ packaged crackers

_____ cutting board

_____ dish rag

_____ fresh eggs

✔ Think About It

You return to your apartment after being gone for a weekend and discover that the power is out. How will you know which foods in the refrigerator are safe to eat?

_____

_____

_____

_____

✓ Apply It

How Do Your Food Safety Habits Stack Up?

Take the following quiz to find out.

How Often Do You	Always	Sometimes	Never
Wash your hands before preparing food?			
Scrub your fruits and vegetables under cold, running water before eating them?			
Use an insulated pouch with an ice pack to carry your perishable lunches and snacks, such as meat-filled sandwiches and/or yogurt and cheese?			
Wash your hands after using the bathroom?			
Throw out refrigerated leftovers after four days?			
Chop raw vegetables on a clean chopping board rather than the one you just used for raw meat, fish, or poultry?			
Use a thermometer to determine if the meat or poultry is done cooking?			

What changes do you need to make to ensure that your foods are safe?

_____

_____

✓ Test It

1. To thrive, bacteria need

    a. sodium, potassium, and fluid.

    b. time, a dark environment, and yeast.

    c. nutrients, moisture, and 40°F to 140°F.

    d. a host, a parasite, and nutrients.

2. The "4 Cs" of food safety include combating cross-contamination, cleaning, cooking, and

   a. covering.

   b. chilling.

   c. clipping.

   d. coordinating.

Who Protects Your Food and How Do They Do It?

✓ Know It

Match each agency to its food supply and safety responsibility.

_____ 1. safety and labeling of meat, poultry, and eggs

_____ 2. safety of all foods except meat, poultry, and eggs

_____ 3. safety of the environment—air and water quality

_____ 4. protecting against plant and animal pests and diseases

_____ 5. monitors disease outbreaks, keeps statistics

_____ 6. coordinates research, surveillance, inspection, outbreak responses, and educational activities

_____ 7. combined effort of the CDC, USDA, and FDA to conduct ongoing monitoring of foodborne illnesses

_____ 8. network of government and public health laboratories that use DNA fingerprinting

a. Animal and Plant Health Inspection Service (APHIS)

b. FoodNet

c. Food and Drug Administration (FDA)

d. PulseNet

e. Environmental Protection Agency (EPA)

f. Food Safety Initiative (FSI)

g. USDA Food Safety and Inspection Service (FSIS)

h. Centers for Disease Control (CDC)

✔ Find It

Unscramble the terms described to find methods of food preservation.

heating to destroy pathogens

AAEIIOUTTRZNPS

— — — — — — — — — — — — — —

heating and packaging food in
airtight containers

AICNNNG

— — — — — — —

additionally heating already
canned foods

EORRTT AIGNNNC

— — — — — —   — — — — — — —

killing pathogens with a
radiant energy source

AAIIIORRTDN

— — — — — — — — — —

changes composition of the
air in a package

EIIODDFM AAEEOSRMPTH AAIGGKPCN

— — — — — — — —   — — — — — — — — —

— — — — — — — — —

✔ Think About It

After visiting a local farmer's market, your mother is convinced that she should purchase unpasteurized
milk directly from a farmer. She said that many nutrients are lost in the pasteurization process. What do
you think of pasteurization?

_____

_____

✔ Apply It

List food items you purchased on your last grocery shopping trip. Determine the type of food preservation method used.

Food Item	Preservation Technique

What was the primary food preservation technique used among the food items you purchased?

_____

_____

✔ Test It

1. The government agency that ensures the safety of foods besides meat, poultry, and eggs is the

   a. FDA.

   b. USDA.

   c. FSIS.

   d. EPA.

2. The food preservation technique that changes the air composition in a package is

   a. HPP.

   b. irradiation.

   c. MAP.

   d. retort canning.

What Are Food Additives and How Are They Used?

✓ Know It

Match each term to the appropriate description.

_____ 1. substances added to food that affect quality, flavor, freshness, and/or safety

_____ 2. having prior approval

_____ 3. meat preservation giving luncheon meat a pink color

_____ 4. history of being safe

_____ 5. prevents browning and inhibits growth of microbes

_____ 6. common flavor enhancer

a. GRAS

b. sulfites

c. prior-sanctioned

d. additive

e. MSG

f. nitrates

✓ Find It

Complete the chart of commonly used food additives.

Additive	Function	Used In
guar gum, lecithin, pectin		baked goods, processed cheese, salad dressings
	improve/maintain nutritive value	breads, cereals, flour, milk
ascorbic acid, BHA, BHT, sodium nitrite	maintain palatability and wholesomeness	
citric acid, sodium bicarbonate, yeast		breads, cookies, cakes
caramel, FD&C red no. 40	enhance color	

✓ Think About It

Your friend is sensitive to sulfites. How can she be sure that the salad bar in the cafeteria doesn't have sulfites added to the fresh produce?

_____

_____

_____

✓ Apply It

Examine the food items in your cupboard and identify at least five food additives. Look these up on the Generally Recognized as Safe (GRAS) list on the FDA's website, www.fda.gov.

Additive	Facts from the FDA Website

What did you learn about the additives?

_____

_____

_____

✓ Test It

1. Vitamin C is added to cut fruit to
   a. improve nutritional quality.
   b. improve consistency.
   c. add color.
   d. prevent premature browning.

2. The use of food additives is regulated by the
   a. USDA.
   b. EPA.
   c. FDA.
   d. CDC.

What Are Toxins and Chemical Agents?

✓ Know It

First fill in the letters for the terms defined. Then transfer each numbered letter to the heading below.

__ __ __ __ __ __   __ __ __   __ __ __ __ __ __ __ L   __ __ __ __ __ __
3 5 13 4 2 8   1 2 10   6 9 7 12 4 6 1   1 11 7 2 3 8

__ __ __ __ B __ __ __ __ __ __   drugs that kill or slow the growth of bacteria
1 2 3 4   4 5 3 4 6 8

P __ __ __ __ __ __ __ __ __   substance that kills pests, rodents, or fungi
  7 8 3 4 6 4 10 7

__ __ R B __ __ __ __ __   substance that kills or controls weeds
9 7   4 6 4 10 7

F U __ __ __ __ __ __ __   chemical used to kill mold
    2 11 4 6 4 10 7

__ __ R __ __ __   __ __ __ __ __   chemicals occurring naturally that contaminate fish
12 1   4 2 7   3 5 13 4 2

__ __ R __ __ __ __ __ __ __ __ __   substance thought to cause cancer
6 1   6 4 2 5 11 7 2 4 6

__ __ U R __ __ __ __ __ __   toxin that affects the nerves
2 7   5 3 5 13 2 8

__ R __ W __ __   __ __ R __ __ __ __   essential for normal growth and development
11 5   3 9   9 5   12 5 3 7

✔ Find It

Check the techniques that help reduce pesticides in foods.

_____   soak fruits and vegetables in soapy water

_____   wash fruits and vegetables under running water

_____   avoid frozen meat products

_____   trim visible fat off of meat

_____   limit fish meals

_____   eat only canned vegetables

_____   avoid dairy products

_____   eat a variety of foods

✔ Think About It

The co-op sells milk that advertises it is "rbST free." Does this make the product a healthier purchase? Why or why not?

_____

_____

✔ Apply It

1. Some consumer groups believe that the FDA and EPA should require labeling of pesticides used in or on food products. What do you think?

_____

_____

2. What products would you avoid if you knew this information?

_____

_____

3. Do you think the average consumer would find this information helpful? Why or why not?

_____

_____

✓ Test It

1. Chemicals such as hormones, antibiotics, and _____ are intentionally given to live-stock and used in agriculture.

   a. neurotoxins

   b. pesticides

   c. carcinogens

   d. toxins

2. Pesticides used to kill microorganisms are

   a. herbicides.

   b. antimicrobials.

   c. fungicides.

   d. biopesticides.

What Is Organic and How Do You Find Organic Foods?

✓ Know It

Circle the correct answer of the choices given.

1. The popularity of organic foods has recently (declined *or* soared).

2. The (National Organic Standards Board *or* Food and Drug Administration) sets specific standards for food labeled as organic.

3. Organic foods (are *or* are not) free of all pesticides.

4. The USDA (has *or* has not) found that organic foods are safer or nutritionally superior to conventionally grown foods.

5. Organic foods generally (do *or* do not) cost more than those that are conventionally grown.

✔ Find It

Check the items below that are considered organic food production.

_____ bioengineering   _____ hormone-free animals

_____ synthetic pesticides   _____ crop rotation

_____ antibiotic-free poultry   _____ synthetic fertilizers

_____ irradiation

✔ Think About It

Will buying produce only at farmer's markets guarantee that the products purchased are organically produced? How could you tell for sure?

_____

_____

✔ Apply It

At a grocery store, look for food products with the USDA Organic seal.

Product	Type of Product (Produce, Packaged, Meat, Dairy, etc.)

1. What foods were most likely to be labeled organic?

_____

_____

_____

2. Did you find these food items throughout the store?

_____

_____

_____

✔ Test It

1. Organically produced foods are generally
   a. free of all pesticides.
   b. safer than conventionally grown foods.
   c. nutritionally superior to conventionally grown foods.
   d. more costly than conventionally grown foods.

2. If a label displays the USDA Organic seal, the food contains at least _____ percent organic ingredients.
   a. 50
   b. 70
   c. 95
   d. 100

What Is Biotechnology and Why Is It Used?

✔ Know It

Match each term to the appropriate description.

_____ 1. application of biological technique to alter genetic makeup

_____ 2. two plants are crossbred to produce desirable traits

_____ 3. cell with its genetic makeup altered

_____ 4. biological technique that manipulates genes to produce a targeted, modified effect

_____ 5. organisms that have been genetically engineered to contain both original and foreign genes

a. genetically modified

b. biotechnology

c. genetically modified organism

d. genetic engineering

e. plant breeding

✔ Find It

Check all of the following that are products of technology.

_____ apples

_____ cotton

_____ canola

_____ domesticated pets

_____ soybeans

_____ human infants

_____ wheat

_____ cheese

✔ Think About It

Some opponents of genetic engineering (GE) voice fears of introduction of allergens into the food supply. Do you think this likely to occur? Why or why not?

_____

_____

✔ Apply It

1. Mandatory labeling of genetically engineered foods is required in Europe, Japan, Australia, and New Zealand. The United States and Canada do not require labeling of these products. Do you think they should?

    _____

    _____

2. Would it make a difference to the average consumer?

    _____

    _____

✔ Test It

1. Genetically engineered foods are regulated by
    a. the GE, GMO, and CDC.
    b. Europe, Japan, and Australia.
    c. the State Health Department.
    d. the FDA, USDA, and EPA.

2. A cell that has its genetic makeup altered
    a. is genetically modified.
    b. is genetically engineered.
    c. is irradiated.
    d. may be carcinogenic.

What Is Bioterrorism and How Can You Protect Yourself?

✓ Know It

Fill in the blanks using the following terms.

water   tampering   food   chemical   biological   bioterrorism

1. The use of a biological or chemical agent to threaten or kill an individual is known as

    _____.

2. Potential targets for bioterrorism are _____ and

    _____ supplies.

3. Food can be contaminated with a _____ or

    _____ toxin.

4. The deliberate contamination of food is referred to as food _____.

✓ Find It

Check the agencies that play a role in food biosecurity.

_____   Department of Homeland Security

_____   Federal Emergency Management Agency (FEMA)

_____   Food and Drug Administration (FDA)

_____   College Health Service

_____   State Health Department

_____   U.S. Department of Agriculture (USDA)

✔ Think About It

A man was not happy with the current teachings in the church he was attending. He intentionally contaminated a casserole served at a church gathering. A number of people became sick. Is this an example of bioterrorism?

_____

_____

✔ Apply It

Navigate through the FDA website, www.fda.gov. List highlights of the FDA's work toward biosecurity.

_____

_____

✔ Test It

1. Government agencies have made _____ a national priority.

    a. genetically modified foods

    b. biotechnology

    c. bioterrorism

    d. health care

2. Food can be the primary agent of bioterrorism by being contaminated with

    a. a biological chemical or toxin.

    b. GMOs.

    c. irradiation.

    d. sulfites and nitrates.

Two Points of View

Can Organic Go Large Scale?

Read two professionals' opinions on this topic at the end of the chapter in your textbook, then consider the following questions:

1. Briefly, define organic.

   _____

   _____

2. Why are organic foods currently popular?

   _____

   _____

3. Does "organic" have anything to do with the size of the food production operation?

   _____

   _____

4. How about distribution?

   _____

   _____

5. Should only small family or cooperative farms be allowed to produce and label organically grown foods?

   _____

   _____

6. Can Wal-Mart be part of the organic movement? Is this good or bad? Why?

   _____

   _____

7. Is "big brand" bad?

_____

_____

8. Where do you purchase organically produced foods?

_____

_____

9. Why do you make purchases there?

_____

_____

Hunger at Home and Abroad

What Is Hunger and Why Does It Exist?

✔ Know It

Match each term to the appropriate description.

_____ 1. physical need for food

_____ 2. chronic inability to satisfy basic food needs

_____ 3. poor nutrition

_____ 4. country advanced in industrial capability and economic productivity

_____ 5. country having a low level of economic productivity

_____ 6. lack of food due to natural occurrences

a. underdeveloped

b. famine

c. malnutrition

d. developed

e. food insecurity

f. hunger

✔ Find It

Check countries in the list below that are considered underdeveloped.

_____   Japan

_____   Ethiopia

_____   Haiti

_____   Mexico

_____   Hong Kong

_____   United States

_____   Yemen

_____   Sierra Leone

✔ Think About It

Could college students face food insecurity? What are possible reasons for such circumstances?

_____

_____

✔ Apply It

If you found yourself in a situation of food insecurity, what community resources are available to you? List resources and their contact information.

Community Resource	Address	Phone Number

✔ Test It

1. The physical need for food is
   a. famine.
   b. hunger.
   c. food insecurity.
   d. malnutrition.

2. Examples of underdeveloped countries include
   a. China, New Zealand, and Brazil.
   b. Hong Kong, Angola, and Saudi Arabia.
   c. Yemen, Haiti, and Ethiopia.
   d. Argentina, Denmark, and Canada.

What Causes Hunger?

✔ Know It

Complete the crossword puzzle.

Across
4 severe shortage of food
7 more people than natural resources can support
9 drought, flood, crop disease
10 sick

Down
1 lack of a job
2 fighting
3 unfair treatment due to race or gender
5 little household income
6 boycotts used to apply political pressure
8 lack of a home

✔ Find It

*Use a **D** to mark possible causes of hunger in the United States. Use a **W** to mark possible causes of global hunger. Some factors may apply to both.*

_____   overpopulation

_____   poverty

_____   single mothers

_____   women

_____   political sanctions

_____   discrimination

_____   unemployment

_____   lack of distribution

✔ Think About It

Prepare two shopping lists similar to textbook Table 15.1.

Grocery store:			Date of study:		
Meal	**Low-Cost Shopping List**	**Cost**	**Healthy Shopping List**		**Cost**
Breakfast	Frozen Waffles (10)		Cereal (10 oz)		
	Syrup (12 oz)		Skim Milk (1 gal)		
	Fruit Punch (1 gal)		Orange Juice (1 gal)		
Snack	Potato Chips (1 lb)		Natural Popcorn (1 lb)		
Lunch	Bologna (1 lb)		Solid White Tuna (1 lb)		
	White Bread (1 lb)		Whole-Wheat Bread (1 lb)		
Dinner	Pasta Sauce with Meat (1 lb)		Chicken Breast (1 lb)		
	Pasta (1 lb)		Broccoli (1 lb)		
Dessert	Ice Cream (½ gal)		Strawberries (2 lbs)		
TOTALS					

✔ Apply It

Complete the Self-Assessment below.

Are You at Risk for Hunger?

Take the quiz below to find out if you are at risk for hunger.
In the past 12 months:

1. Have you ever run out of money to buy food?
Yes ☐ **No** ☐

2. Have you ever eaten less than you felt you should because there was not enough money to buy food or enough food to eat?
Yes ☐ **No** ☐

3. Have you ever completely depleted your food supply because there was not enough money to buy replacement groceries?
Yes ☐ **No** ☐

4. Have you ever gone to bed hungry because there was not enough food to eat?
Yes ☐ **No** ☐

5. Have you ever skipped meals because there was not enough money to buy food?
Yes ☐ **No** ☐

6. Have you ever relied on a limited number of foods to feed yourself because you were running out of money to buy food?
Yes ☐ **No** ☐

Answers

If there are zero yes replies, you are not hungry. If there are one to three yes replies, you are at risk for hunger. If there are four or more yes replies, you are classified as "hungry."

Source: Adapted from The Community Childhood Hunger Identification Project Survey, July 1995; R. E. Kleinman et al., Hunger in Children in the United States: Potential Behavioral and Emotional Correlates, Emotional Correlates, *Pediatrics* 101 (1998): 3–10.

Did you anticipate the outcome? Do you think any of your answers could change? Why?

_____

_____

✔ Test It

1. Those at greatest risk of food insecurity in the United States include
   a. households in rural areas.
   b. households headed by single men.
   c. households with children.
   d. suburban households.

2. _____ is a serious problem worldwide.
   a. Gender inequity
   b. Famine
   c. Armed conflict
   d. Wastefulness in agricultural practices

What Are the Effects of Hunger?

✔ Know It

Match the physical symptoms of starvation to the organ or system affected.

_____ 1. chip, decay, loosen   a. GI tract

_____ 2. circulatory difficulties   b. mouth and lips

_____ 3. rashes, sores, peeling   c. teeth and gums

_____ 4. diarrhea or constipation   d. eyes

_____ 5. weakness, atrophy   e. muscles

_____ 6. dry, sore   f. skin

_____ 7. poor vision   g. hair

_____ 8. unhealthy and discolored   h. heart

✔ Find It

Check the five primary causes of childhood death in developing countries (according to the World Health Organization).

_____ poverty   _____ civil unrest

_____ diarrhea   _____ malaria

_____ single mothers   _____ malnutrition

_____ acute respiratory infections   _____ measles

✔ Think About It

The Dominican Republic, a vacation destination location, is on the same island as Haiti, one of the poorest underdeveloped countries in the world. What do you think of this dichotomy?

_____

_____

✔ Apply It

Research the work done by the World Health Organization (WHO) against hunger. List at least three points you learned from visiting the WHO website.

_____

_____

_____

✔ Test It

1. Growth stunting is manifested in

   a. teenage athletes.

   b. pregnant women.

   c. early childhood.

   d. the elderly.

2. Whenever infant and child mortality rates are high, _____, which perpetuates the cycle of malnutrition.

   a. elderly death rates are low

   b. pregnancy rates are low

   c. birth rates are low

   d. birth rates are high

How Can We Eradicate Hunger?

✔ Know It

Fill in the blanks using the terms below.

> bioengineered   safe water   education   land ownership   biotechnology
>
> food fortification

1. _____ can create crops with increased yields, pest resistance, and improved quality.

2. Some staple crops can be _____ to contain nutrients to help alleviate common nutrient deficiencies.

3. _____ provides incentive for improved land decisions regarding irrigation, crop rotation, and soil management.

4. Providing food is important to reducing hunger, but _____ is equally important.

5. _____ can bring extra nutrients to staple foods.

6. _____ can increase economic and career opportunities as well as build self-esteem and confidence.

✔ Find It

The curriculum for international education is different in the developing world than in the developed world. Check the components needed in international education.

_____ literacy

_____ technical knowledge

_____ biotechnology

_____ health education

_____ development of drought-resistant plants

_____ development of natural resources

_____ nutrient fortification

✔ Think About It

Bioengineered "golden rice" is rich in beta-carotene. The populations for which this product is intended, so as to improve their nutritional status, are reluctant to use it. It has a different color and appearance from their customary rice. Some consumer advocacy groups also claim that this product is expensive and takes advantage of the world's poorest cultures to benefit big businesses in the United States. What do you think?

_____

_____

_____

✔ Apply It

Volunteer at a food assistance program in your community. What were your experiences?

_____

_____

_____

✓ Test It

1. The key to ensuring food security worldwide is
   a. providing adequate food.
   b. providing a safe water supply.
   c. developing bioengineered products.
   d. education.

2. _____ play(s) an important role in the economy of most developing countries.
   a. Foreign aid
   b. Agriculture
   c. Locally made handicrafts
   d. Health care

Two Points of View

Why Does Hunger Exist in the United States?

Read two professionals' opinions on this topic at the end of the chapter in your textbook, then consider the following questions:

1. Who is most likely to experience food insecurity in the United States?

   _____

   _____

2. Where is this most likely to occur?

   _____

   _____

3. What factors contribute to hunger among U.S. citizens?

   _____

   _____

4. What could be done to ameliorate this situation?

_____

_____

5. What can the government do to improve food security?

_____

_____

6. Outline what you will do to help alleviate hunger in your community.

_____

_____

_____

Answer Key

Chapter 1

What Drives Our Food Choices?

Know It: 1. b, 2. d, 3. c, 4. a, 5. e

Find It:

Taste and Culture: salty pretzels, rice as a staple, environment

Social Reasons and Trends: bond with others, pre-washed vegetables, holiday dinner

Time and Convenience: instant mashed potatoes, rotis-serie chicken, pre-washed vegetables

Advertising: Got Milk, breakfast cereals

Habits and Emotions: chocolate, bagel for breakfast, celebratory meal

Think About It: 1. social reasons, 2. time and convenience, 3. taste and culture

Test It: 1. b, 2. b

What Is Nutrition and Why Is Good Nutrition so Important?

Know It: 1. c, 2. d, 3. b, 4. e, 5. a

Find It: cancer, stroke, heart disease, diabetes

Think About It: 1. chili con carne, 2. lemonade

Test It: 1. d, 2. c

What Are the Essential Nutrients and Why Do You Need Them?

Know It: 1. macronutrients, 2. micronutrients, 3. calories, 4. organic, 5. inorganic

Find It:

	Energy	Growth, Maintenance, or Structure	Regulate Body Processes	Carbon Containing
Carbohydrate	X	X		X
Protein	X	X		X
Fats	X	X		X
Vitamins			X	
Minerals		X		
Water			X	

Think About It: 1. daily caloric needs; 2. fat/lipid; 3. exercise

Apply It: 108, carbohydrate, 52

Test It: 1. d, 2. c

How Should You Get These Important Nutrients?

Know It: 1. c, 2. b, 3. a, 4. e, 5. d

Find It: 1. carbohydrate, 2. carbohydrate, 3. protein, 4. broccoli, 5. popcorn, 6. broccoli

Think About It: 1. eat more fruits, 2. eat more vegetables, 3. eat whole-grain products

Test It: 1. a, 2. b

How Does the Average American Diet Stack Up?

Know It: increase life expectancy, improve quality of life, promote good health

Find It: Low: vitamin E, calcium, fiber; High: sodium, saturated fat, calories

Think About It: 1. Defined as a rapid spread, development, or growth. 2. Obesity is called an epidemic because the incidence is widespread and growing.

Test It: 1. a, 2. d

What's the Real Deal When It Comes to Nutrition Research and Advice?

Know It: 1. d, 2. i, 3. h, 4. a, 5. g, 6. e, 7. b, 8. f, 9. c

Find It: d, b, a, f, c, e

Think About It: 1. double-blind placebo-controlled study; 2. received water; 3. received a flavored beverage

Test It: 1. c, 2. d

Chapter 2

What Is Healthy Eating and What Tools Can Help?

Know It: 1. b, 2. e, 3. a, 4. c, 5. f, 6. d

Find It: excessive intake of iron, too many calories, drinking sugar-sweetened beverages

Think About It: undernutrition

Test It: 1. a, 2. c

What Are the Dietary Reference Intakes?

Know It: 1. c, 2. d, 3. a, 4. b, 5. g, 6. f, 7. e

Find It: 60, 140, 40, +140

Think About It: you are eating too much fat as compared to carbohydrate and protein; decrease fat/fried foods/spreads and increase carbohydrates and protein.

Test It: 1. b, 2. a

What Are the *Dietary Guidelines for Americans?*

Know It: 1. e, 2. i, 3. b, 4. d, 5. a, 6. f, 7. g, 8. c, 9. h

Find It: 1. Maintaining body weight: a, b, c; 2. Eat more fruits and vegetables: d, f, g; 3. Increase physical activity: b, c; 4. Include low fat dairy products: d, e, f

Think About It: 1. no; lacking in fruits, vegetables, and dairy products

Test It: 1. c, 2. d

What Is a Food Guidance System?

Know It: 1. c, 2. f, 3. a, 4. d, 5. g, 6. e, 7. b

Find It:

Food Group	Calorie Dense	Nutrient Dense
Grains	cookies, pastries	rice, oats, whole-grain cereal
Vegetables	french fries, potato chips	fresh and frozen
Fruit	canned in syrup, drinks	whole, 100% real juice
Milk	ice cream, cheese	low-fat cheese, milk, yogurt
Meat and Beans	luncheon meats, fried products	eggs, lean meat, dried beans and peas

Think About It: nutrient density; fruits, vegetables, dairy foods, lean meat

Think About It, More: Moderate (M): downhill skiing, canoeing, playing baseball, recreational volleyball; Vigorous (V): swimming, hip hop dancing, game of rugby

Test It: 1. c, 2. b, 3. a

What Is a Food Label and Why Is It Important?
Know It:

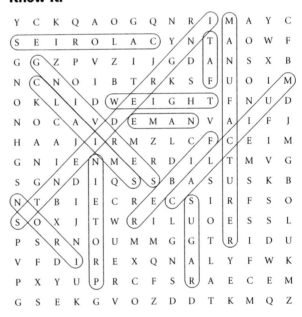

Find It: S, A, A, Q, S, A, Q

Think About It: 1. GoLean; 2. same; 3. GoLean; 4. same; 5. same; 6. GoLean

Test It: 1. d, 2. a

Functional Foods: What Role Do They Play in Your Diet?

Know It: 1. health benefits: a, b, c; 2. animal compounds: a, c; 3. plant chemicals: a, b; 4. treatment of chronic diseases: a, b, c

Find It: P, Z, P, P, Z

Think About It: 1. functional foods; 2. yogurt; 3. the culture is what makes it yogurt, the other products were fortified with a nutrient/chemical

Test It: 1. d, 2. b

Chapter 3

What Makes Eating So Enjoyable?

Know It: 1. a, 2. e, 3. d, 4. c, 5. b

Find It: potato chips = salty, frosting = sweet, chokecherries = bitter, mashed potatoes = umami, lemon juice = sour

Think About It: 1. hunger, 2. appetite, 3. thirst

Test It: 1. a, 2. c

What Is Digestion and Why Is It Important?

Know It: 1. c, 2. e, 3. d, 4. b, 5. a

Find It: mechanical digestion: chew, grind, mouth; chemical digestion: digestive juices, enzymes, stomach, absorbable nutrients

Think About It: mechanical digestion

Test It: 1. d, 2. a

What Happens in the Individual Organs of the GI Tract?

Know It: 1. d, 2. c, 3. e, 4. a, 5. b

Know It, Too: 1. e, 2. d, 3. g, 4. b, 5. a, 6. c, 7. f

Find It: bile, gastrin, enzymes, saliva, mucus, hydrochloric, bicarbonate; DIGESTIVE SECRETIONS

Think About It: 1. macaroni and cheese because it has some fat and a little protein; 2. low-fat milk

Test It: 1. b, 2. a

What Other Body Systems Affect Your Use of Nutrients?

Know It: 1. c, 2. d, 3. a, 4. b

Find It:

Nervous System: hormones, hunger sensation, stop eating

Circulatory System: network of capillaries, carries oxygen and nutrients, removes carbon dioxide, heart and lungs

Lymphatic System: network of capillaries, fat-soluble vitamins, immune system

Excretory System: waste products, urine

Think About It: nervous system

Apply It: 1. you urinate frequently; 2. drink more fluids

Test It: 1. c, 2. d

What Are Some Common Digestive Disorders?

Know It: 1. a, 2. b, 3. c, 4. a, 5. e, 6. b, 7. e, 8. c, 9. b, 10. e

Find It:

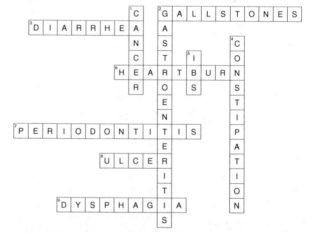

Think About It: heartburn; stay upright, don't lie down; eat smaller meals, eat slower, decrease intake of fat, decrease intake of alcohol, quit smoking.

Test It: 1. b, 2. c

Chapter 4

What Are Carbohydrates and Why Do You Need them?

Know It: 1. c, 2. a, 3. b, 4. b

Find It: apples and oranges, low-fat milk, squash and sweet potato, garbanzo beans, granola

Think About It: cells and brain

Test It: 1. a, 2. d

What Are Simple and Complex Carbohydrates?

Know It:

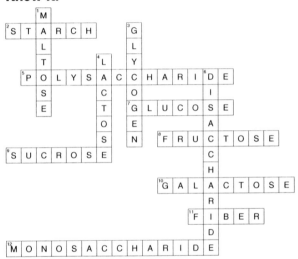

Find It: fructose, glucose, lactose

Find Some More of It: S, I, I, S, S, S

Think About It: 1. fresh fruit, vegetable salad, fruit juice with pulp, 2. will vary

Test It: 1. b, 2. c

Grains, Glorious Whole Grains

Know It: 1. d, 2. f, 3. b, 4. e, 5. a, 6. c

Find It: Bran (high fiber, B vitamins), Endosperm (starch, protein, B vitamins), Germ (unsaturated fat, B vitamins, vitamin E)

Think About It: 1. cracked-wheat flour is high in fiber and rich in antioxidants; the white flour is missing many key nutrients, including B vitamins. White flour has gluten to make a lighter bread product; 2. using only whole grain would make a heavy, dense bread product.

Test It: 1. d, 2. c

What Happens to the Carbohydrates You Eat?

Know It: blood, liver, stomach, intestine, mouth; DIGESTION

Find It: 2, 6, 3, 1, 5, 4

Think About It: 1. lactose intolerance; 2. lactase; 3. may be able to tolerate small amounts of whole milk, cheese, active culture yogurt

Test It: 1. c, 2. c

How Does Your Body Use Carbohydrates?

Know It: 1. d, 2. c, 3. a, 4. b; 1. sugar new; 2. sugar breakdown; 3. sugar new beginning

Find It: 1. glycogenesis: a, b; 2. gluconeogenesis: b; 3. release of glycogen: d; 4. store excess glycogen: a, b, c; 5. release of insulin: d; 6. ketone bodies: c

Think About It: 1. ketosis; 2. recommend another technique for weight reduction—need to include carbohydrate to feed the brain

Apply It: See pages 97 and 98 in your textbook.

Test It: 1. a, 2. b

How Much Carbohydrate Do You Need and What Are Its Food Sources?

Know It: S: fresh fruit, dairy foods, vegetables, and sugar, sweets; C: fresh fruit, whole grains, legumes and beans, vegetables; F: fruit, grains, vegetables, legumes

Find It: chart blanks in order: 2 T hummus 4 g; 1 cup pasta 44 g; ½ cup raisins 65 g; 7 halves walnuts 2 g; 23 g; ¼ cup raisins 32 g

Think About It: 1. could be an adequate menu with a few additions. 2. Would want to know how things are prepared, how big are portion sizes, what is in hobo stew, what kind of bread is used, etc. 3. Suggestions: more fresh fruits and vegetables.

Test It: 1. c, 2. a

What's the Difference Between Natural and Added Sugars?

Know It: keep cookies moist; add to the structure of a dessert bar; help a pie crust to brown when baked; act as a preservative; thicken a sauce; add flavor

Find It: Label 1: corn syrup, apple puree concentrate. Label 2: sugar, molasses, corn syrup, sugar, sugar, corn syrup solids, high-fructose corn syrup, sorbitol, fructose, molasses.

Think About It: 1. similar in calories, carbohydrate, and protein; 2. different in small amount of fat and fiber; 3. Label 1 had over 2 times the sugar. Label 1 is Kelloggs fruit-flavored snack; 4. Label 2 is Quaker Chewy Chocolate Chunk Granola Bar

Test It: 1. d, 2. c

What Are Sugar Substitutes and What Forms Can They Take?

Know It: 1. d, 2. f, 3. b, 4. g, 5. a, 6. c, 7. e

Find It: chewing gum and candy; baked goods; toothpaste; vitamin supplements; beverages

Think About It: PKU is an inborn error of metabolism. People with PKU may need to monitor their use of aspartame. The FDA deems aspartame safe. She can get by without aspartame, check labels, and avoid it.

Test It: 1. b, 2. c

Why Is Fiber so Important?

Know It: 1. b, 2. d, 3. a, 4. e, 5. c

Find It: 1. obesity; 2. heart disease; 3. heart disease and diabetes; 4. diabetes; 5. cancer

Think About It: Eat more fresh fruits and vegetables, drink plenty of fluids, be active.

Test It: 1. c, 2. c

What Is Diabetes Mellitus and Why Is It an Epidemic?

Know It: 1. d, 2. e, 3. a, 4. f, 5. c, 6. b

Find It:

Prediabetes: weight reduction, balanced diet, exercise

Type 1: insulin therapy, self-glucose monitoring, balanced diet and exercise

Type 2: insulin therapy, medication, weight reduction, self-glucose monitoring, balanced diet, exercise

Think About It: 1. Risk factors: obesity, obese parents, parent with diabetes, Native American, African-American, Hispanic, Asian-American, or Pacific Islander descent. 2. Encourage a balanced healthy diet, encourage physical activity

Test It: 1. a, 2. c

What Is Hypoglycemia?

Know It: 1. c, 2. d, 3. a, 4. b

Think About It: eat small well-balanced meals throughout the day

Test It: 1. b, 2. c

Chapter 5

What Are Lipids and Why Do You Need Them?

Know It:

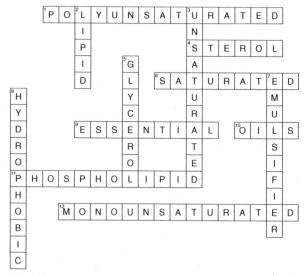

Find It: 1. The three types of lipids are: triglyceride, phospholipid, and sterol. 2. Lipids are used in cooking

and food preparation for satiety, tender meats, flaky texture, and aroma and flavor. 3. Lipids are essential in the body for insulation, energy storage, and transport proteins.

Think About It: Lecithin is not essential. The body can make what it needs.

Apply It:

Lipid	Number of Double Bonds	Solid or Liquid
saturated	none	solid
monounsaturated	one	liquid
polyunsaturated	2 or more	liquid
linoleic acid	2 or more	liquid

Test It: 1. d, 2. a

What Happens to the Fat You Eat?

Know It: STOMACH AND SMALL INTESTINE, bile, diglyceride, monoglyceride, lymph, lipoproteins, chylomicron, lipase

Find It: 2, 4, 3, 1, 5

Think About It: high-fat food—meat, dairy products, fried foods

Why? Because the gallbladder releases bile; without it, fat metabolism is affected.

Apply It:

Lipoprotein	Triglyceride %	Phospholipid %	Cholesterol %	Protein %	Function
chylomicron	90	3	5	2	transports fat through lymph system
VLDL	60	18	12	10	delivers fat made in the liver to the tissues
LDL	10	15	50	25	delivers cholesterol to cells
HDL	5	25	20	50	removes cholesterol from cells

Test It: 1. c, 2. d

How Does Your Body Use Fat and Cholesterol?

Know It: sources of energy, cushions organs, part of cell membranes, carries vitamins A, D, and K

Find It:

Linoleic acid: essential fatty acid, eicosanoids, blood clotting, vegetable oils

Alpha-linolenic acid: essential fatty acid, omega-3 fatty acid, eicosanoids, cell membranes, fish

Cholesterol: made by the liver; cell membranes, sex hormones

Think About It: 1. fish oil supplements could contain toxic amounts of chemicals and vitamins A and D; 2. to be heart healthy, eat fish, balanced diet, exercise.

Test It: 1. a, 2. c

How Much (and What Types of) Fat Should You Eat?

Know It:

Fats to include: linoleic acid, alpha-linolenic acid, monounsaturated fats

Fats to limit: cholesterol, saturated fats, *trans* fats

Find It: 1. 34%, 2. 40%, 3. 33%, 4. fat, calories, 5. fat, calories, 6. refined carbohydrates

Think About It: 1. the menu appears high in fat, low in fresh produce. 2. The menu is designed to be calorically dense for activity and ability to carry. 3. answers vary.

Test It: 1. b, 2. b

What Are the Best Food Sources of Fats?

Know It: Unsaturated: vegetable oils, tree nuts (walnuts), flaxseed, and wheat germ. Saturated: meat, whole dairy products, coconut and palm oil, commercially made baked goods.

Find It: eggs, milk, shrimp, cheese, ice cream, turkey

Think About It: 1. 1,120 calories from fat; 2. this is equal to 40% of the total calories; 3. need to reduce fat intake

Test It: 1. d, 2. b

What Is *Trans* Fat and Where Do You Find It?

Know It: 1. c, 2. d, 3. a, 4. b

Find It: resistance to rancidity, better texture, decrease costs, replace saturated fat

Find More: breakfast cereals, commercially baked goods, hydrogenated shortening, potato chips, salad dressing, animal products. Major contributor of *trans* fat: commercially baked goods; second: animal products

Think About It: better choices: vegetable pizza, carrot sticks, applesauce, minestrone soup, mineral water

Test It: 1. b, 2. d

What Are Fat Substitutes and How Can They Be Part of a Healthy Diet?

Know It: 1. b, 2. c, 3. a, 4. e, 5. d

Find It: 1. muffins, 2. shake, 3. potatoes, 4. cookies, 5. cake

Think About It: these would be a matter of personal choice; explanation of choice is needed

Test It: 1. c, 2. a

What Is Heart Disease and What Increases Your Risk?

Know It: 1. b, 2. g, 3. d, 4. f, 5. c, 6. e, 7. a

Find It: Controllable: excess body weight, insulin sensitivity, smoking, physical inactivity, low HDL cholesterol, high LDL cholesterol, hypertension. Uncontrollable: age, type 1 diabetes, family history of disease, gender. Nutrition related: excess body weight, insulin sensitivity, type 1 diabetes, low HDL cholesterol, high LDL cholesterol, hypertension

Think About It: 1. poor diet, smoking, obesity. 2. balanced diet, exercise, weight reduction, stop smoking.

Test It: 1. b, 2. c

What Is High Blood Cholesterol and What Can You Do to Lower It?

Know It: increase unsaturated fat, limit *trans* fat, include fruits and vegetables daily, eat fish, include nuts

Find It: egg yolk, hamburger, low-fat milk, chicken, chicken noodle soup

Think About It: high cholesterol, high saturated fat, lacking in phytochemicals, high protein

Test It: 1. d, 2. b

Chapter 6

What Are Proteins?

Know It:

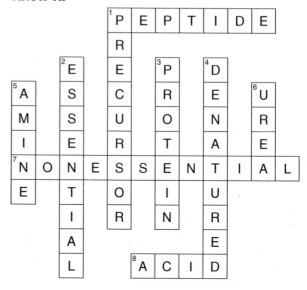

Find It: egg, milk, pork chop

Think About It: would not choose any of these amino acids to be added because they are all non-essential

Test It: 1. c, 2. b

What Happens to the Protein You Eat?

Know It: 1. e, 2. g, 3. b, 4. a, 5. c, 6. d, 7. f, 8. h

Find It: 3, 1, 5, 2, 4

Think About It: too much protein is not good. This is a sign that the kidneys are being overtaxed.

Test It: 1. b, 2. b

How Does Your Body Use Proteins?

Know It: 1. e, 2. g, 3. b, 4. f, 5. a, 6. c, 7. d

Find It:

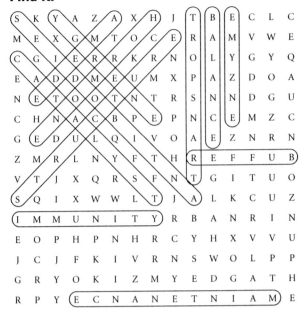

Think About It: 1. fluid balance, 2. immunity

Test It: 1. d, 2. b

How Much Protein Do You Need and What Are Protein-Rich Food Sources?

Know It: 1. d, 2. g, 3. a, 4. b, 5. e, 6. c, 7. f

Find It: Complete: low-fat milk, pork chop, salmon, Colby cheese. Incomplete: green beans, hummus, whole-grain bread, pear, peanut butter, baked potato, rye crackers, rice

Think About It: possible examples: hummus + whole-grain bread; cheese + potato; rye crackers + peanut butter; rice + beans

Test It: 1. d, 2. b

What Happens if You Eat Too Much or Too Little Protein?

Know It: phrase: PROTEIN DEFICIENCY; terms: malnutrition, kwashiorkor, marasmus, PEM, energy, children

Find It: due to too much protein: increased risk of heart disease, osteoporosis, kidney stones, obesity; due to too little protein: compromised immune status, loss of cells in GI tract, osteoporosis, emaciated appearance, edema

Think About It: yes, marasmus (same as anorexia nervosa)

Test It: 1. c, 2. a

How Do Vegetarians Meet Their Protein Needs?

Know It: 1. d, 2. e, 3. a, 4. b, 5. c

Find It: Lacto-ovo-vegetarian: goat's-milk cheese, orange, tempeh, yogurt, broccoli, sunflower seeds, soy milk, omelet, fruit juice, whole-grain bread, ice cream, sorbet; Lacto-vegetarian: all except omelet and tuna fish; Semi-vegetarian: all;

Vegan: orange, tempeh, broccoli, sunflower seeds, soy milk, fruit juice, whole-grain bread, sorbet

Think About It: 1. sounds boring, little variety; suggest main entrees that are plant based; 2. examples: macaroni and cheese, spinach lasagna, soy burger, etc.

Test It: 1. c, 2. b

Chapter 7

What Are Vitamins?

Know It: organic, essential, amount needed is small, fat soluble, water soluble, stored in the body, excreted easily from the body

Know It, Too: Water soluble: thiamin, riboflavin, vitamin C, folate, niacin, vitamin B_6, vitamin B_{12}, biotin. Fat soluble: vitamin A, vitamin D, vitamin E, vitamin K

Find It: keep produce at room temperature, freeze produce, refrigerate produce, store in airtight containers, microwave vegetables, shop for produce frequently and use quickly, steam vegetables

Think About It: any could be an option depending on the reason given.

Test It: 1. c, 2. a

Vitamin A

Know It: 1. d, 2. f, 3. a, 4. g, 5. b, 6. c, 7. h, 8. e

Find It: squash, yam, sweet potato, milk, cheese, eggs, green leafy vegetables, carrots

Think About It: eating too many foods with carotenoids

Test It: 1. c, 2. b

Vitamin E

Know It: 1. alpha-tocopherol, 2. anticoagulant, 3. antioxidant, 4. hemorrhage

Find It: vegetable oil, wheat germ, nuts and seeds, soy milk, avocado

Think About It: vitamin E supplements are not needed

Apply It: 1. iceberg head lettuce + spinach, broccoli; 2. whole-grain crackers + peanut butter; 3. raisins, chocolate; 4. chips + almonds; 5. oatmeal + wheat germ

Test It: 1. a, 2. c

Vitamin K

Know It: 1. synthesized by intestinal bacteria, 2. found in green plants, 3. coenzyme, 4. Inadequate, 5. no, 6. decreases

Find It: spinach, olive oil, asparagus, cabbage, intestinal bacteria, margarine

Think About It: infants do not have intestinal bacteria. Vitamin K is given to increase blood clotting

Apply It:
1. crusty french bread + oil and vinegar; 2. iceberg lettuce + broccoli, cabbage; 3. carrots + salad dressing; 4. potato + margarine, asparagus

Test It: 1. a, 2. b

Vitamin D

Know It: 1. sunlight, 2. inactive, 3. inactive, 4. hormone, 5. less frequent, 6. prevent, 7. rickets, 8. do not include

Find It: increased consumption of soft drinks, concern over skin cancer, limited outdoor activities, air pollution

Think About It: Minneapolis, MN; Detroit, MI; Seattle, WA; Des Moines, IA; Boston, MA; Grand Forks, ND; Madison, WI; Big Sky, MT

Apply It:
1. granola, fruit + yogurt; 2. mixed salad greens + salmon; 3. fresh berries + fortified cereal; 4. coffee + milk

Test It: 1. b, 2. d

Thiamin (B$_1$)

Know It: 1. was the first B vitamin discovered, 2. nerve function, 3. energy metabolism, 4. beriberi

Find It: pork loin, whole-grain cereal, enriched rice; pork loin provides the most thiamin.

Think About It: yes, in cases of excessive alcohol intake and poor diet

Apply It: 1. yogurt + cereal; 2. vegetable beef soup with pasta; 3. mashed potatoes + peas, pork; 4. toast + oatmeal

Test It: 1. c, 2. b

Riboflavin (B$_2$)

Know It: 1. is sensitive to light, 2. energy metabolism, 3. affects the tissues of the throat, mouth, and tongue

Find It: fresh greens, cheese pizza, scrambled egg, enriched cereal, yogurt

Think About It: pizza, macaroni and cheese, pasta, cereals, milk

Test It: 1. a, 2. b

Niacin (B$_3$)

Know It: 1. is used in high doses as a drug to treat high cholesterol, 2. healthy skin cells, functioning of the digestive system, 3. is called pellagra

Find It: Cheerios, pasta, chicken, corn, enriched rice

Think About It: 1. flushing, vasodilation, prominent vessels are desirable in competition; 2. could be a dangerous practice. 3. It is not likely that you have pellagra; you may have dry skin in need of lotion.

Apply It: 1. whole-wheat bread + chicken breast; 2. M & M's + peanuts; 3. pasta + beef tips; 4. salad greens + peppers, tuna fish flakes

Test It: 1. d, 2. c

Vitamin B$_6$

Know It: 1. b, 2. d, 3. a, 4. c

Find It: broccoli, baked potato, banana, hamburger, chicken, spinach, kidney beans

Think About It: supplements of B$_6$ have not been shown to alleviate the symptoms of PMS. Get adequate B$_6$ from the diet.

Apply It: 1. milk + cereal; 2. whole-grain bread + peanut butter; 3. apples + bananas; 4. salad greens + kidney beans, chicken breast

Test It: 1. a, 2. d

Folate

Know It: 1. e, 2. b, 3. g, 4. a, 5. c, 6. d, 7. f

Find It: orange juice, green leafy vegetables, whole-grain bread, pasta, cold cereal

Think About It: 1. $80\,\mu g \times 1.7 = 136$ DFE

2. tomato sauce, green vegetables

Apply It: 1. milk + crackers; 2. lettuce + chickpeas, spinach, broccoli; 3. chicken + asparagus; 4. yogurt + cereal

Test It: 1. a, 2. b

Vitamin B$_{12}$

Know It: 1. cobalamin, 2. water, 3. can, 4. protein, 5. diminishes, 6. animal

Find It: milk, tuna fish, pork chop, shrimp, egg

Think About It: 1. pernicious anemia, 2. diet is not likely to make the situation better because intrinsic factor is needed for B$_{12}$ absorption.

Apply It: 1. broccoli + cheese; 2. pineapple + cottage cheese; 3. bread + chicken breast; 4. boiled potatoes + fish

Test It: 1. c, 2. d

Vitamin C

Know It: 1. ascorbic acid, 2. coenzyme, 3. antioxidant, 4. plant, 5. scurvy

Find It: tomato, potato, broccoli, watermelon

Think About It: 1. Erick may not need the supplement; Julia's dose is too high. 2. Erick probably does not risk side effects; 3. Julia risks nausea, diarrhea, and kidney stones.

Apply It: 1. apple, pear + grapefruit, cantaloupe; 2. turkey sandwich with tomatoes; 3. frozen yogurt + strawberries; 4. corn flakes + orange juice

Test It: 1. c, 2. d

Pantothenic Acid and Biotin

Know It: 1. water, 2. energy, 3. easily meet, 4. intestinal bacteria, 5. a wide variety of food products

Find It: eggs, peanut butter, bran flakes, milk, mozzarella cheese, turkey

Think About It: unsafe to use raw egg white, also too much could bind biotin

Test It: 1. a, 2. d

Are There Other Important Nutrients?

Know It: 1. c, 2. a, 3. d, 4. b

Find It:

Choline: dairy products, eggs, peanuts

Carnitine: meat, dairy products

Inositol: plant foods

Think About It: 1. You don't need a carnitine supplement; it is not an essential nutrient, as your body can synthesize what it needs. 2. Don't waste your money.

Test It: 1. b, 2. a

What Are Antioxidants?

Know It: 1. d, 2. g, 3. b, 4. f, 5. a, 6. e, 7. c

Find It: orange juice, green tea, lettuce, tomato, onion, apple, coleslaw, soy burger, broccoli, red wine

Think About It: 1. yes, 2. adequate diet with vitamins C, E, and beta-carotene

Test It: 1. d, 2. b

How Should You Get Your Vitamins?

Know It: calcium in orange juice, vitamins A and D in milk, vitamin C in a fruit drink, folic acid in cereal

Find It: a woman planning a pregnancy, someone on a low-calorie diet, alcoholic, someone with multiple food allergies, a child who is a picky eater

Test It: 1. c, 2. b

Chapter 8

What Is Water and Why Is It so Important?

Know It: 1. d, 2. a, 3. f, 4. e, 5. b, 6. c

Find It: 1. average adult male, 2. muscular athlete, 3. growing child, 4. average male, 5. male with 14 percent body fat

Think About It: 105.4 pounds

Test It: 1. b, 2. d

What Does Water Do in Your Body?

Know It: Phrase: essential roles of water: solvent, transport, temperature, lubricant, cushion.

Find It: taste and saliva, amniotic fluid around a fetus, evaporation of sweat, swelling of a sprained ankle

Think About It: humidity prevents the cooling mechanism of sweat; only sweat that evaporates is able to cool the body

Test It: 1. b, 2. c

What Is Water Balance and How Do You Maintain It?

Know It:

Crossword answers:
- 1 Down: HYPONATREMIA
- 2 Across: DEHYDRATION
- 3 Down: OSMOSIS
- 4 Down: THIRST
- 5 Down: BALANCE
- 6 Down: DIURETIC
- 7 Across: ANTIDIURETIC
- 8 Across: INSENSIBLE

Find It: I: juice, oatmeal and bread, coffee, tea, energy metabolism. O: kidneys, urine, large intestine, sweat, lungs

Think About It: The scale may show a lower weight due to dehydration; this is not fat loss.

Test It: 1. a, 2 d

How Much Water Do You Need and What Are the Best Sources?

Know It: 1. c, 2. a, 3. e, 4. d, 5. f, 6. b

Find It: 1. cooked oatmeal, 2. fruit juice, 3. milk, 4. eggs

Think About It: no need to change pattern; after this amount of time you have become tolerant to the caffeine and it no longer acts as a diuretic

Test It: 1. b, 2. b

What Are Minerals and Why Do You Need Them?

Know It: 1. organic, 2. inorganic, 3. bioavailability, 4. major, 5. trace

Find It: M: chloride, potassium, calcium, magnesium, sodium, sulfur, phosphorus.

T: iron, zinc, copper, chromium, manganese, fluoride, selenium. Mineral in greatest quantity in the body: calcium.

Think About It: this supplement contains the upper level of trace minerals and not much calcium

Test It: 1. d, 2. d

Sodium

Know It: 1. electrolyte, 2. fluid balance, 3. flavor, 4. preservative, 5. processed foods, 6. natural sources, 7. hypertension.

Find It: 1. pretzel, 2. tomato juice, 3. pickle, 4. hot dog, 5. cottage cheese

Think About It: flavor, preservative

Test It: 1. a, 2. b

You and Your Blood Pressure

Know It: 1. hypertension, 2. increases, 3. systolic, 4. diastolic, 5. silent

Find It: Controllable: physical activity, alcohol intake, stress, body weight, sodium intake. Not controllable: family history, age, race, gender

Think About It: medication can only do so much; it is possible to eat your way through the medication. He could also become active, lose weight, and follow the DASH diet.

Test It: 1. c, 2. d

Potassium

Know It: 1. fluid balance, 2. blood buffer, 3. muscle contraction, 4. nerve conduction, 5. blood pressure, 6. bone health

Find It: banana, milk, potato, tomato, hamburger, kidney beans

Think About It: could be dangerous; grandmother could develop hyperkalemia.

Apply It: 1. toast + orange juice; 2. turkey, cheese + spinach sandwich; 3. Cheerios, nuts + yogurt; 4. lettuce + many vegetables

Test It: 1. b, 2. a

Calcium

Know It: 1. bones, teeth, 2. bones, 3. blood, muscles, other tissues, 4. blood pressure, cancer, kidney stones, obesity, 5. osteoporosis, 6. hypercalcemia.

Find It: yogurt, cottage cheese, bok choy, tofu, broccoli

Think About It: consume with a meal, limit dose to 500 mg at a time, look for the USP symbol on the label

Apply It: 1. cereal + low-fat milk; 2. pineapple + yogurt; 3. turkey, bread + reduced-fat cheese; 4. iceberg lettuce + broccoli, kale

Test It: 1. a, 2. c

Phosphorus

Know It: 1. a major mineral, mostly in bones, 2. bones and teeth, cell membranes, energy metabolism, genetic material, 3. termed hyperphosphatemia, a problem for people with kidney disease, leads to bone loss

Find It: chicken, orange juice, milk, broccoli, peas, strawberries, cereal. Most phosphorus is found in milk.

Think About It: Soda pops are replacing more nutrient-dense foods and beverages.

Apply It: 1. whole-wheat bread + tuna sandwich; 2. ice cream + strawberries; 3. banana + raisin bran; 4. baked potato + almonds

Test It: 1. c, 2. d

Magnesium

Know It: 1. is found in bones, is in intracellular fluid, 2. metabolism of the energy nutrients, building healthy muscles, facilitating nerve function, maintaining healthy bones, regulating heart beat, 3. occurs with supplement use, affects the gastrointestinal tract

Find It: peanut butter, wheat germ, cottage cheese, banana, almonds

Think About It: dependence can develop; can result in chronic diarrhea

Apply It: 1. yogurt + almonds, cereal; 2. lettuce + spinach; 3. salsa + black beans; 4. whole-grain crackers + peanut butter

Test It: 1. b, 2. c

Chloride and Sulfur

Know It: Cl: stomach acid, electrolyte in extracellular fluid, blood buffer, preservative. S: thiamin, biotin, pantothenic acid, amino acids, preservative

Find It: 1. table salt, 2. animal and plant foods, 3. 3,600 mg, 4. not set

Think About It: 2100 mg

Test It: 1. d, 2. c

Osteoporosis: Not Just Your Grandmother's Problem

Know It: 1. c, 2. d, 3. a, 4. b

Find It: Caucasian or Asian-American, family history of bone fractures, smoking, consume less than 3 cups of dairy products daily

Think About It: 1. Reducing risk of osteoporosis can occur at any age. 2. Yes, typical college students can be at risk of osteopenia. 3. Because they may have a poor diet and lack physical activity.

Test It: 1. b, 2. a

Iron

Know It: 1. d, 2. f, 3. a, 4. b, 5. c, 6. e

Find It: H: sirloin steak, tuna fish. N: breakfast cereal, raisins, brown sugar/molasses, cast-iron cookware, tofu, black beans

Think About It: 1. Given the symptoms, you might suspect iron-deficiency anemia. 2. She could be certain of the diagnosis by visiting a physician and having a simple blood hemoglobin test. 3. Possible causes could be heavy menstrual bleeding and a poor diet.

Apply It: 1. eggs + enriched wheat toast; 2. milk + cereal; 3. raisins, almonds + tangerine; 4. baked potato + salsa, chicken

Test It: 1. a, 2. b

Copper

Know It: 1. enzymes, proteins, 2. iron, 3. generate, 4. blood clotting, 5. rare

Find It: walnuts, black beans, turkey, raisins, wheat germ, hot cocoa, liver, oatmeal

The highest amount of copper is found in liver.

Think About It: You do not need to worry about copper toxicity if a child swallows a penny because pennies are no longer made out of copper.

Apply It: 1. cocoa + milk; 2. rice + seafood; 3. raisins + walnuts; 4. whole-grain pita + black beans, salsa

Test It: 1. d, 2. b

Zinc

Know It: needed for protein synthesis, reduces inflammation of skin wounds, has a role in taste acuity, reduces risk of age-related macular degeneration, vegetarians have a higher need

Find It: 1. wheat germ, 2. flank steak, 3. shrimp, 4. yogurt

Think About It: the phrase is a play on words for the purpose of advertising

Apply It: 1. crackers + tuna fish; 2. oatmeal + raisins; 3. yogurt + mixed nuts; 4. pasta + peas

Test It: 1. b, 2. d

Selenium

Know It: 1. proteins, 2. enzymes, 3. antioxidant, 4. fight, 5. selenosis, 6. Keshar disease

Find It: 1. chicken, 2. roast beef, 3. egg, 4. Brazil nuts

Think About It: Taking a selenium supplement is probably not prudent. A varied diet can provide adequate sources of selenium.

Apply It: 1. pasta + broccoli; 2. bagel + cheese; 3. apple + peanut butter; 4. almonds + cottage cheese

Test It: 1. c, 2. a

Fluoride

Know It: repairs tooth enamel, reduces bacterial acid in the mouth, protects teeth, is a component of saliva

Find It: teeth are pitted and mottled, teeth are resistant to decay, infants and children are at most risk, can be caused by eating toothpaste

Think About It: Fluoride treatments may be needed. They help to build a barrier on teeth that prevents bacterial decay.

Test It: 1. d, 2. a

Chromium

Know It: 1. trace, essential, 2. increase, 3. has not, 4. rare, 5. adequate

Find It: 1. chicken, 2. turkey, 3. broccoli, 4. apple

Think About It: Hopefully you would not choose the free sample of chromium picolinate. It has not been scientifically proven to have any effect on fat or lean tissue.

Test It: 1. c, 2. d

Iodine

Know It: 1. d, 2. c, 3. a, 4. e, 5. b

Find It: drinking water, milk, pickles, canned soup

Think About It: No. Adding too much iodine would impair the thyroid gland.

Test It: 1. a, 2. d

Manganese

Know It: activates many enzymes, involved in metabolism of energy nutrients, helps bone formation, cinnamon is a good source

Find It: 1. raisin bran cereal, 2. spinach, 3. pineapple, 4. pecans

Think About It: This level of manganese is too high. Hopefully you would not choose to use it because it is a hazardous level of this mineral.

Apply It: 1. whole-wheat toast + cinnamon; 2. rice + pine nuts, chickpeas; 3. frozen yogurt + pineapple; 4. vegetable soup + lentils

Test It: 1. b, 2. d

Molybdenum

Know It: 1. trace, 2. amino acids, 3. enzymes, 4. adequate

Find It: whole-grain bread, chick peas, brown rice, lentils, garbanzo beans

Test It: 1. b

Other Minerals: Arsenic, Boron, Nickel, Silicon, and Vanadium

Know It: 1. c, 2. e, 3. b, 4. a, 5. d

Find It: dairy products: a, b; meat, poultry: a; grain products: a, d, d; nuts, legumes: b, c; vegetables: b, d; parsley and black pepper: e

Think About It: No, large amounts of these minerals are toxic. Labeling is not required by the FDA.

Test It: 1. a, 2. b

Chapter 9

What Is Alcohol and How Is It Made?

Know It: 1. d, 2. f, 3. e, 4. a, 5. c, 6. b

Find It: contains food energy, legally sold in the United States, expensive as compared to bottled water, can be toxic, beer is made from grains

Think About It: water, grain, sugar, and yeast and a method for distillation

Apply It: Common uses include drinking alcohol, alcohol used in cleaning or sterilizing.

Test It: 1. d, 2. c

Why Do People Drink Alcohol?

Know It: celebration, relaxation, pleasure, escape reality, religious tradition

Find It: Women: 4 oz Chablis wine, 12 oz hard lemonade, 1 oz brandy.
Men: 22 oz tall tap beer, 2 oz tequila, 4 oz Chablis wine

Think About It: maybe, it depends on lifestyle choices for activity, foods, and stress

Test It: 1. b, 2. c

What Happens to Alcohol in the Body?

Know It: 1. cannot, 2. Twenty, 3. stomach, 4. less, 5. Muscular, more, 6. liver, 7. correlates, 8. depressant.

Find It: 1. female eating a cheeseburger, 2. 18-year-old male, 3. 160-pound male, 4. an athlete, 5. student who had pizza lunch

Think About It: 1. This is not good advice; all alcohol has to be metabolized.

2. Yes, depending on the volume ingested the night before.

Test It: 1. c, 2. b

How Can Alcohol Be Harmful?

Know It:

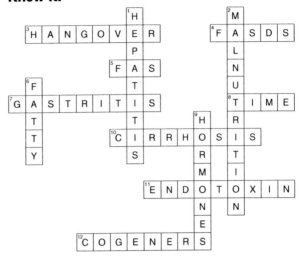

Find It: 1. hangover, 2. diuretic, 3. electrolyte imbalance, 4. osteoporosis, 5. cancer, 6. nutrient absorption, 7. liver disease

Think About It: tolerance to alcohol can be built up, but it is still metabolized

Test It: 1. d, 2. c

What Are Alcohol Abuse and Alcoholism?

Know It: 1. d, 2. b, 3. a, 4. g, 5. f, 6. e, 7. c

Find It: needs more alcohol for it to have an effect, has symptoms of withdrawal if alcohol intake is halted, craves alcohol, cannot control or limit intake

Think About It: 1. suggest counseling and AA to your roommate; 2. ultimately, the decision to get help is up to her; 3. get counseling and attend Al Anon yourself.

Test It: 1. b, 2. c

Who Should Avoid Alcohol and What Is Moderate Drinking?

Know It: pregnant or lactating women, children, those taking over-the-counter medications, those taking prescription medications, operators of heavy equipment, school bus drivers

Find It: 12 oz brewed beer, 12 oz light beer, 5 oz red wine

Think About It: No, this is an example of binge drinking.

Test It: 1. d, 2. b

Chapter 10

What Is Weight Management and Why Is It Important?

Know It: 1. d, 2. a, 3. e, 4. b, 5. c

Find It: heart disease, type 2 diabetes, arthritis, sleep apnea, some cancers

Think About It: Possible causes of weight loss include intestinal disorders, excessive caloric restriction, increased physical activity, and emotional distress.

Test It: 1. b, 2. c

How Do You Know If You're at a Healthy Weight?

Know It:

```
 1S  U  2B  C  U  T  3A  N  E  O  U  S
 K      O               B
 I      D               S
 N      P               O
 F      O               R
 O      D      4I  M  P  E  D  A  N  C  E
 L                       T
 D            5C     6V  I  S  C  E  R  A  L
             E          I
             N      7B   M  I
             T          E
 8U  N  D  E  R  W  A  T  E  R
             A          R
             L          Y
```

Find It: Techniques that estimate percent of body fat: skinfold thickness, bioelectrical impedance, underwater weighing, BodPod, dual X-ray absorptiometry. None of these techniques are direct measurements, they are all estimates.

Think About It: No, the football player may have a lot of muscle mass and may not have extra body fat. BMI may not be accurate for him.

Test It: 1. b, 2. c

What Is Energy Balance and What Determines Energy Needs?

Know It: 1. c, 2. f, 3. a, 4. b, 5. g, 6. e, 7. d

Find It: a. muscle mass, b. infant, c. man, d. tall individual, e. Caucasian, f. fever/illness, g. feasting, h. espresso coffee, i. both hot and cold.
2. BMR would be affected equally by going to a hot environment or going to a cold environment.

Think About It: 1. Your friend would become acclimated to a colder environment; 2. smoking is a negative health behavior. She should try good nutrition and exercise to manage her weight.

Test It: 1. d, 2. a

What Are the Effects of an Energy Imbalance?

Know It: P: going to coffee break every day; stopping for a mocha latte; drinking three beers every evening. **N:** walking instead of driving; skipping breakfast and lunch; eating only fruit

Find It: 1. pretzels, 2. bagel, 3. iced tea, 4. carrots, 5. fruit cocktail

Think About It: your choice of foods is high in calories

Test It: 1. d, 2. c

What Factors Are Likely to Affect Body Weight?

Know It: satiety, ghrelin, leptin, cholecystokinin, thermogenesis

Find It: examples of NEAT: swinging your feet while sitting, tapping a pencil on a table, folding laundry, playing a video game

Test It: 1. b, 2. d

How Can You Lose Weight Healthfully?

Know It: eat more fruits and vegetables, eat multiple small meals during the day, eat moderate amounts of protein, cut back on full-fat dairy products, walk for 30 minutes each day

Find It: eat as much meat as you can stuff in, don't eat anything white, the exact combination of foods is important, only eat fruits in the morning, lose up to seven pounds in a week, you must buy this newly discovered formula along with a diet

Think About It: some possible suggestions could include: cheese omelet with toast, pancakes without butter, hamburger with lettuce and tomato, carrots and low-fat milk, baked chicken, baked potato

Test It: 1. c, 2. a

How Can You Maintain Weight Loss?

Know It: ate frequent small meals, maintained a high level of physical activity, monitored calorie intake

Find It: 1. breakfast at home, 2. walking around the building during breaks, 3. walking on a treadmill, 4. bringing lunch from home, 5. meeting for a hike and picnic

Think About It: 1. Your aunt is experiencing weight cycling. 2. Advice would be to eat frequent small meals, monitor calories, weigh weekly, be positive, and exercise.

Test It: 1. c, 2. a

How Can You Gain Weight Healthfully?

Know It: eat nutrient-dense foods, eat more often during the day, drink beverages with calories

Find It: 1. granola, 2. applesauce, 3. chocolate low-fat milk, 4. fruit-flavored low-fat yogurt, 5. chicken salad, 6. mashed potato

Think About It: Your skinny friend could be just as challenged and frustrated as someone trying to lose weight.

Apply It: Carry snacks such as granola and applesauce cups.

Test It: 1. c, 2. a

Extreme Measures for Extreme Obesity

Know It: 1. e, 2. d, 3. g, 4. b, 5. f, 6. c, 7. a

Find It: 1. very low-calorie diets a, b, d; 2. gastric bypass surgery a, d, d, e; 3. gastric banding a, d, e; 4. liposuction e, 5. orlistat f

Think About It: Your classmate should try diet, exercise and behavior modification.

Test It: 1. d, 2. c

What Is Disordered Eating and How Can You Identify It?

Know It: a. anorexia nervosa: weight less than 85% of expected weight, fear of gaining weight, overconcern with body shape and size, absence of menstrual cycles; b. bulimia nervosa: recurrent episodes of binge eating, recurrent purging, overconcern with body shape and weight; c. eating disorder not otherwise specified: recurrent episodes of binge eating, binging without purging, eating at night

Find It: vomiting after eating, excessive exercise, use of laxative, fasting

Think About It: 1. You could suspect bulimia nervosa in your roommate. 2. Suggest that she contact the student health service for help.

Test It: 1. d, 2. c

How Are Disordered Eating Behaviors Treated?

Know It: 1. a, 2. b, 3. a, 4. c, 5. a, 6. c

Find It: developing a meal plan, identifying foods that trigger a binge, determining when hungry, food and mood journaling

Think About It: Your friend needs a multidisciplinary approach with trained professionals.

Test It: 1. c, 2. b

Chapter 11

What Is Fitness and Why Is It Important?

Know It: 1. e, 2. h, 3. c, 4. g, 5. a, 6. b, 7. i, 8. f, 9. d

Find It: increased HDL cholesterol, less visceral fat, increased insulin sensitivity, reduced risk of osteoporosis, enhanced immune system

Think About It: 1. This does not sound like a total fitness program. 2. It may help with flexibility. 3. All other components of fitness are lacking.

Test It: 1. a, 2. d

What Does a Fitness Program Look Like?

Know It: aerobic, stroke volume, intensity, duration, frequency

Find It: C: jogging 3 miles, paddling a kayak, step aerobic class. M: weight lifting, moving furniture, ballet. F: Pilates, ballet

Think About It: 1. RPE 16–17 (very hard). 2. Advice: start slow, moderate pace, build slowly, gradually increase intensity or duration.

Test It: 1. c, 2. a

How Are Carbohydrate, Fat, and Protein Used during Exercise?

Know It:

```
    ¹L  O  ²A  D  I  N  G
    ³L      N                    ⁴A  T  ⁵P
    A       A                    A      R
    C   ⁶A  E  R  O  B  I  C            O
    T       R                           T
    I       O              ⁷F           E
    ⁸C  A  R  B  O  H  Y  D  R  A  T  E
            I                    T      I
    ⁹M  U  S  C  L  E                   N
```

Find It: C: running up five flights of stairs, biking for ten miles, chopping wood. P: recovering from a marathon. F: folding laundry, low-level aerobics.

Think About It: No. It is the calories that count.

Test It: 1. a, 2. c

What Vitamins and Minerals Are Important for Fitness?

Know It: 1. a, 2. d, 3. b, 4. e, 5. c

Find It: muscle strain or sprain, iron-deficiency anemia, blood clotting, muscle contraction, bone loss

Think About It: stop any excessive bleeding, good nutrition and possibly iron supplementation

Test It: 1. c, 2. d

How Does Fluid Intake Affect Fitness?

Know It: 1. d, 2. e, 3. a, 4. c, 5. b

Find It: water, Gatorade

Think About It: The soccer team could use a day off, lighter training, and increased fluid consumption.

Test It: 1. c, 2. d

Can Dietary Supplements Contribute to Fitness?

Know It:

heading: ERGOGENIC AID

creatine, caffeine, anabolic steroid, growth hormone, erythropoietin, blood doping

Find It: a: dehydration; b: death, androgenic effects, tumor development; c: reduce body fat in trained athletes, acromegaly; d: increase blood viscosity, death

Think About It: development of diabetes, atherosclerosis, hypertension, acromegaly

Test It: 1. d, 2. b

Chapter 12

How Does a Baby Begin Developing?

Know It: 1. f, 2. c, 3. g, 4. e, 5. a, 6. d, 7. b

Find It: 4, 5, 1, 3, 2

Think About It: smoke, chemicals, alcohol

Test It: 1. d, 2. a

What Nutrients and Behaviors Are Most Important for a Healthy Pregnancy?

Know It: Positive behaviors: a variety of fruits and vegetables, snacking on nuts, lean meat products. Negative behaviors: smoking, botanicals, coffee, tuna fish for lunch daily, wine with dinner, socializing in a smoke-filled bar

Find It: 1. d, 2. f, 3. a, 4. b, 5. c, 6. e, 7. g

Think About It: avoid alcohol, avoid secondhand smoke, eat more fruits and vegetables, moderate weight

Test It: 1. b, 2. c

In the First Trimester

Know It: 1. d, 2. b, 3. g, 4. c, 5. f, 6. e, 7. a

Find It: small frequent meals, carbohydrates—rice, pasta, crackers, vitamin B_6, potato chips and lemonade, ginger ale

Think About It: small frequent meals, high in carbohydrates, sip on ginger ale

Test It: 1. c, 2. b

In the Second Trimester

Know It: 1. b, 2. e, 3. d, 4. a, 5. c

Find It: obesity, over 25 years old, history of high glucose levels, African-American or Native American, previously given birth to a very large baby

Think About It: avoid contact and high-impact activities, including downhill skiing and weight lifting, continue yoga, avoid excessive fatigue, stay hydrated

Test It: 1. c, 2. c

In the Third Trimester

Know It: difficulty climbing stairs, problems sleeping, constipation, heartburn, low back pain

Find It: H: small, frequent meals, avoid spicy and highly seasoned foods. C: whole grains, fruits and vegetables, plenty of fluid, beans and nuts

Think About It: get off the couch, stay upright after eating, eat small frequent meals, avoid spicy and seasoned foods

Test It: 1. d, 2. b

What Special Concerns Might Younger or Older Mothers-to-Be Face?

Know It: T: high nutrient needs for growth, pregnancy-induced hypertension, low birth weight baby. O: pregnancy-induced hypertension, gestational diabetes, problems conceiving

Find It: adequate folic acid, avoid caffeine, avoid alcohol, eat fruits and vegetables, include low-fat dairy

Think About It: good meal planning, fruits and vegetables, low-fat dairy, lean meats, adequate calories, avoid caffeine and alcohol

Test It: 1. c, 2. c

What Is Breast-Feeding and Why Is It Beneficial?

Know It: 1. b, 2. e, 3. f, 4. d, 5. a, 6. c

Find It: promotes bonding with the mother, reduces risk of chronic diseases, provides immune protection, helps intellectual development

Find It, Too: quicker return to prepregnancy size and shape, reduced risk of breast cancer, promotes bonding with the infant, saves money

Think About It: even for a short time, breast-feeding is beneficial to mom and baby. And she may be able to nurse before and after work and express milk during the work day.

Test It: 1. a, 2. c

What Are the Best Dietary and Lifestyle Habits for a Breast-Feeding Mother?

Know It: 1. 13, 2. 500, 3. fat, 4. about the same

Find It: caffeine, alcohol, contaminants that the mother consumes, nicotine, flavors from spicy foods, fluid

Think About It: the alcohol will be passed through the breast milk to the infant. This is not a healthy practice.

Test It: 1. d, 2. b

When Is Formula a Healthy Alternative to Breast Milk?

Know It: AIDS, receiving chemotherapy or radiation, taking prescription medications, infant has galactosemia

Find It: 1. commercial formula, 2. much, 3. low, high, 4. poorly absorbed

Think About It: Not much. Formulas now must meet strict FDA standards.

Test It: 1. a, 2. b

What Are the Nutrient Needs of an Infant and Why Are They so High?

Know It: suckles, able to hold head up, able to sit up, able to chew food, feeds self

Find It: 5, 2, 1, 4, 3

Think About It: 1. Prepared infant foods may not be needed. 2. handy, easy to use, ready to use, can be stored, can be used for travel. 3. cost

Test It: 1. b, 2. d

When Are Solid Foods Safe?

Know It: 1. c, 2. a, 3. b, 4. d, 5. e

Find It: egg, peanut butter, chocolate, strawberries, cow's milk

Think About It: The milk is replacing solid foods in the child's diet. Hopefully, the scene is different at home.

Test It: 1. b, 2. c

A Taste Could Be Dangerous: Food Allergies

Know It: 1. b, 2. a, 3. g, 4. e, 5. c, 6. d, 7. f

Find It: store-bought cookies, ice cream, frozen dairy treats, crackers, seafood salad, frozen entrees, school lunch

Think About It: Help administer the Epi-pen injection. Call 911 for emergency help.

Test It: 1. c, 2. a

Chapter 13

Young Children's Nutritional Needs and Issues

Know It: 1. e, 2. c, 3. a, 4. b, 5. f, 6. d

Find It: chewing gum, popcorn, hot dog, raw vegetables, rock, coin. To modify the foods to be acceptable for a four-year-old: cut up the hot dog and cook the vegetables. Popcorn and gum should not be offered.

Think About It: Possible ideas could include adding cut-up fruit, serving the cereal with milk, adding a dollop of yogurt, or making cereal bars.

Test It: 1. b, 2. c

School-Aged Children's Nutritional Needs and Issues

Know It: access to vending machines, overweight parents, drinking sports beverages, lack of fruits and vegetables, television viewing, large portion sizes

Find It: calories, fats, protein, calcium, iron, vitamin C

Think About It: This is an unfortunate situation that needs some different agreed-upon management techniques.

Test It: 1. d, 2. c

Adolescents' Nutritional Needs and Issues

Know It: 1. Adolescence, 2. menarche, 3. epiphyseal plate, 4. calcium, 5. Both obesity and disordered eating

Find It: desire for independence, defiance of authority, desire for individuality, media influences, peer influences

Think About It: There is a possibility of damaging the epiphyseal plate in adolescents if activity is long or strenuous—as in marathon running.

Test It: 1. d, 2. b

Older Adults' Nutritional Issues

Know It: need fewer calories, fiber needs decrease, lose ability to absorb vitamin B_{12}, need for calcium increases

Find It: 1. f, 2. b, 3. d, 4. c, 5. e, 6. a

Think About It: Problems you might expect to see in a poorly nourished elderly individual include constipation, dehydration, anemia, and a depressed immune system.

Test It: 1. b, 2. a

What Additional Challenges May Older Adults Face?

Know It: 1. d, 2. f, 3. a, 4. b, 5. e, 6. c

Find It: limited finances, lack of transportation, inability to prepare food, tooth or gum disease, alcohol abuse, multiple medications

Think About It: 1. Seniors are likely to go to familiar community settings to socialize. 2. Other services could include educational programming, socialization with games, brief health checks like blood pressure

Test It: 1. c, 2. a

Drugs, Food, and Drug-Herb Interactions

Know It: 1. c, 2. f, 3. a, 4. d, 5. b, 6. e

Find It: calcium, garlic, grapefruit juice, vitamin K, fish oil, vitamin E, niacin

Think About It: avoid aged cheese, smoked fish, yogurt, and red wine

Test It: 1. b, 2. d

Chapter 14

What Causes Foodborne Illness and How Can It Make You Sick?

Know It:

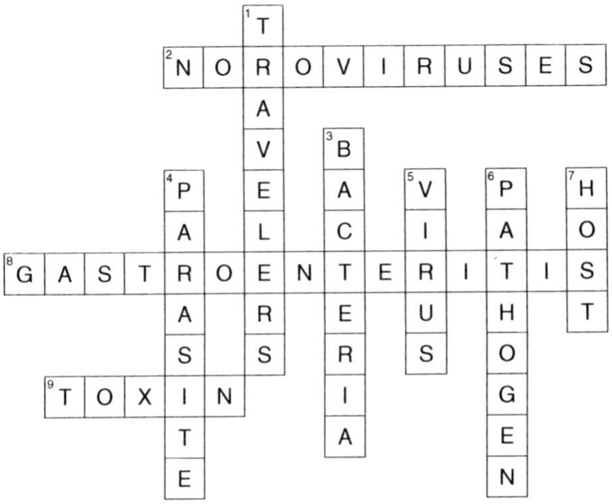

Find It: infants, elderly, someone being treated with chemotherapy or radiation, someone with AIDS, pregnant women, residents of a group home

Think About It: To avoid traveler's diarrhea use only bottled water, eat only fully cooked foods, wash all produce, and avoid tap water.

Test It: 1. d, 2. b

What Can You Do to Prevent Foodborne Illness?

Know It: 1. e, 2. g, 3. a, 4. f, 5. c, 6. d, 7. b

Find It: your hands, kitchen counter, kitchen sink, cutting board, dish rag

Think About It: You won't know what foods are safe. Throw it all out and sanitize the refrigerator.

Test It: 1. c, 2. b

Who Protects Your Food and How Do They Do It?

Know It: 1. g, 2. c, 3. e, 4. a, 5. h, 6. f, 7. b, 8. d

Find It: pasteurization, canning, retort canning, irradiation, modified atmosphere packaging

Think About It: Purchasing unpasteurized milk is not safe. Raw milk can contain *Salmonella*, *E. coli*, and *Listeria monocytogenes*.

Test It: 1. a, 2. c

What Are Food Additives and How Are They Used?

Know It: 1. d, 2. c, 3. f, 4. a, 5. b, 6. e

Find It:

Additive	Function	Used In
guar gum, lecithin, pectin	maintain or improve consistency	baked goods, processed cheese, salad dressings
ascorbic acid, folate, thiamin, iron, niacin, riboflavin, vitamins A & D, zinc	improve/maintain nutritive value	breads, cereals, flour, milk
ascorbic acid, BHA, BHT, sodium nitrite	maintain palatability and wholesomeness	bread, cake mixes, cheese, frozen and dried fruit, margarine, meat, potato chips
citric acid, sodium bicarbonate, yeast	light texture, control pH	breads, cookies, cakes
caramel, FD&C red no. 40	enhance color	baked goods, cheese, candies, soft drinks, soup, yogurt

Think About It: The salad bar should be labeled if sulfites are used. Check about this with the food service manager.

Test It: 1. d, 2. c

What Are Toxins and Chemical Agents?

Know It: heading: TOXINS AND CHEMICAL AGENTS; terms: antibiotics, pesticide, herbicide, fungicide, marine toxin, carcinogenic, neurotoxin, growth hormone

Find It: wash fruits and vegetables under running water, trim visible fat off of meat, limit fish meals, eat a variety of foods

Think About It: The FDA views rBST as safe for human use.

Test It: 1. b, 2. b

What Is Organic and How Do You Find Organic Foods?

Know It: 1. soared, 2. National Organic Standards, 3. are not, 4. has not, 5. do

Find It: synthetic pesticides, antibiotic-free poultry, hormone-free animals, crop rotation

Think About It: Just because something is sold at a farmer's market does not guarantee it is organically produced. Ask the farmer about his/her techniques.

Test It: 1. d, 2. c

What Is Biotechnology and Why Is It Used?

Know It: 1. b, 2. e, 3. a, 4. d, 5. c

Find It: apples, cotton, canola, soybeans, wheat, cheese

Think About It: The FDA strictly monitors genetically modified and engineered foods. GE is expensive; a company won't invest in a product with limited use.

Test It: 1. d, 2. a

What Is Bioterrorism and How Can You Protect Yourself?

Know It: 1. bioterrorism, 2. food, 3. water, 4. biological, 5. chemical, 6. tampering

Find It: Department of Homeland Security, Federal Emergency Management Agency, Food and Drug Administration, State Health Department, Department of Agriculture

Think About It: Yes, this is food tampering and is considered bioterrorism.

Test It: 1. c, 2. a

Chapter 15

What Is Hunger and Why Does It Exist?

Know It: 1. f, 2. e, 3. c, 4. d, 5. a, 6. b

Find It: Ethiopia, Haiti, Yemen, Sierra Leone

Think About It: Yes, college students could face food insecurity for a variety of reasons including no job, high cost of tuition, lack of family support, and desire to do it on their own.

Test It: 1. b, 2. c

What Causes Hunger?

Know It:

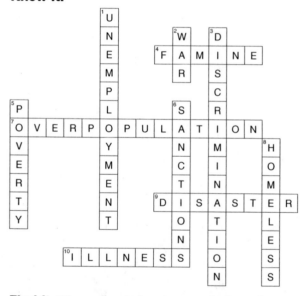

Find It: W: overpopulation, poverty, single mothers, women, political sanctions, discrimination, lack of distribution. **D:** poverty, women, unemployment

Test It: 1. c, 2. a

What Are the Effects of Hunger?

Know It: 1. c, 2. h, 3. f, 4. a, 5. e, 6. b, 7. d, 8. g

Find It: diarrhea, acute respiratory infections, measles, malaria, malnutrition

Test It: 1. c, 2. d

How Can We Eradicate Hunger?

Know It: 1. biotechnology, 2. bioengineered, 3. land ownership, 4. safe water, 5. food fortification, 6. education

Find It: literacy, technical knowledge, health education, development of natural resources

Test It: 1. d, 2. b